MEDAL MATHS

Year 5

Practice Textbook

By
Nicola McGee

Medal Maths Practice Textbook Year 5
   This is not a photocopiable book.

Rising Stars UK Ltd., 76 Farnaby Road, Bromley, BR1 4BH
www.risingstars-uk.com

Published 2004
Text, design and layout © Rising Stars UK Ltd.

Editorial: Tanya Solomons
Concept design: Marc Burville-Riley
Design: Clive Sutherland
Illustrations: © Clive Sutherland and Marc Burville-Riley
Cover design: Marc Burville-Riley

British Library Cataloguing in Publication Data
A CIP record for this book is available from the British Library.

ISBN 1-904591-42-6

Printed by Wyndeham Gait, Grimsby, UK.

Contents

How to use this book

Medal Maths has been created to provide pupils with a complete series of questions to support the whole National Numeracy Strategy Framework. There are three different levels of questions: Bronze, Silver and Gold.

Answers are available in the Medal Maths Teacher's Book Year 5.

Explanations
Explanations and examples are given for each objective to support children working independently.

Medal Standard	Objective Level
Bronze Medal Questions	NNS Year 4
Silver Medal Questions	NNS Year 5
Gold Medal Questions	NNS Year 6

Pupil's Notes

Practice and more practice is the best method for getting results and improving your performance in Maths.

For the best results:

a) Read the explanation.

b) Complete the questions at the most appropriate level.

c) Use the hints and tips to help you.

d) See if you can complete the next level of questions!

Bronze Medal Questions
These questions are set at the level expected for Year 4 as presented by the NNS Framework.

Silver Medal Questions
These questions are set at the expected level for Year 5 as presented by the NNS Framework.

How to use this book

National Numeracy Strategy
Every area of the NNS is covered (including all the Mental Maths objectives).

Objective
Each objective is covered through an explanation, three levels of questions and hints and tips.

---

6 Numbers and the number system

Place value

We can write numbers in figures or words.
Each digit has a different **place value**.

Figures	Words
624	Six hundred and twenty-four
1352	One thousand, three hundred and fifty-two

 Bronze

a) Write these numbers in words:
1. 624 = ☐ hundred and ☐☐
2. 385 = ☐ hundred and ☐☐
3. 726 = ☐ hundred and ☐☐
4. 3241 = ☐ thousand ☐ hundred and ☐☐
5. 6284 = ☐ thousand ☐ hundred and ☐☐

b) Write these numbers in figures:
1. Nine hundred and fifty-two
2. Two hundred and seventy-nine
3. Seven hundred and eleven
4. One thousand, two hundred and twenty-four
5. Three thousand, five hundred and fifty-six

 Silver

a) Write these numbers in words:
1. 3452 = ☐ thousand ☐ hundred and ☐☐
2. 5365 =
3. 9728 =
4. 13245 = ☐ thousand ☐ hundred and ☐☐
5. 56284 =

b) Write these numbers in figures:
1. Four thousand, two hundred and sixty-five
2. Seven thousand, six hundred and seventy-eight
3. Nine thousand, seven hundred and forty-two
4. Fifteen thousand, three hundred and eighty-nine
5. Thirty-three thousand, eight hundred and twenty-six

Gold

a) Write these numbers in words:
1. 17645 = ☐ thousand ☐ hundred and ☐☐
2. 38685 =
3. 567983 = ☐ thousand ☐ hundred and ☐☐
4. 983712 =
5. 702456 =

b) Write these numbers in figures:
1. One hundred thousand, five hundred and twenty-nine
2. Seven hundred thousand, two hundred and eighty-six
3. Four hundred and thirty-two thousand, seven hundred and ninety-four
4. Eight hundred and seventy-nine thousand, five hundred and sixty-four
5. Six hundred and fifty-seven thousand, seven hundred and ninety-one

Gold Medal Questions
These questions are set at the level expected for Year 6 as presented by the NNS Framework.

Questions
There are approximately 3000 questions covering all the NNS Objectives.

Training Tips

 Be careful when reading numbers with a zero (306 reads three hundred and six).

 Remember that the value of a digit depends on its place in the number.

Hints and Tips
Hints and tips support lower ability students and help to consolidate learning.

Sport Theme
The sport theme is often used within the questions to put the maths into context.

Place value

We can write numbers in figures or words.

Each digit has a different **place value**.

Figures	Words
624	Six hundred and twenty-four
1352	One thousand, three hundred and fifty-two

Bronze

a) Write these numbers in words:

1. 624 = ☐ hundred and ☐☐
2. 385 = ☐ hundred and ☐☐
3. 726 = ☐ hundred and ☐☐
4. 3241 = ☐ thousand ☐ hundred and ☐☐
5. 6284 = ☐ thousand ☐ hundred and ☐☐

b) Write these numbers in figures:

1. Nine hundred and fifty-two
2. Two hundred and seventy-nine
3. Seven hundred and eleven
4. One thousand, two hundred and twenty-four
5. Three thousand, five hundred and fifty-six

Silver

a) Write these numbers in words:

1. 3452 = ☐ thousand ☐ hundred and ☐☐
2. 5365 =
3. 9728 =
4. 13245 = ☐ thousand ☐ hundred and ☐☐
5. 56284 =

b) Write these numbers in figures:

1. Four thousand, two hundred and sixty-five
2. Seven thousand, six hundred and seventy-eight
3. Nine thousand, seven hundred and forty-two
4. Fifteen thousand, three hundred and eighty-nine
5. Thirty-three thousand, eight hundred and twenty-six

Gold

a) Write these numbers in words:

1. 17645 = ☐ thousand ☐ hundred and ☐☐
2. 38685 =
3. 567983 = ☐ thousand ☐ hundred and ☐☐
4. 983712 =
5. 702456 =

b) Write these numbers in figures:

1. One hundred thousand, five hundred and twenty-nine
2. Seven hundred thousand, two hundred and eighty-six
3. Four hundred and thirty-two thousand, seven hundred and ninety-four
4. Eight hundred and seventy-nine thousand, five hundred and sixty-four
5. Six hundred and fifty-seven thousand, seven hundred and ninety-one

 **Training Tips**

 Be careful when reading numbers with a zero (306 reads three hundred and six).

Remember that the value of a digit depends on its place in the number.

Multiply and divide by 10 or 100

When you multiply a number by 10, the digits move one place to the left.

When you multiply a number by 100, the digits move two places to the left.

$6 \times 1 = 6$

$6 \times 10 = 60$

$6 \times 100 = 600$

When you divide a number by 10, the digits move one place to the right.

When you divide a number by 100, the digits move two places to the right.

$6 \div 1 = 6$

$60 \div 10 = 6$

$600 \div 100 = 6$

Bronze

a) **Multiply these numbers by 10:**

1. $12 \times 10 =$
2. $28 \times 10 =$
3. $36 \times 10 =$
4. $84 \times 10 =$
5. $68 \times 10 =$

b) **Divide these numbers by 10:**

1. $60 \div 10 =$
2. $80 \div 10 =$
3. $250 \div 10 =$
4. $400 \div 10 =$
5. $860 \div 10 =$

c) **Now try these:**

1. $386 \times 10 =$
2. $420 \div 10 =$
3. $862 \times 10 =$
4. $350 \times 10 =$
5. $980 \div 10 =$

Silver

a) **Multiply these numbers by 10 or 100:**

1. $1235 \times 10 =$
2. $285 \times 100 =$
3. $3623 \times 10 =$
4. $8405 \times 100 =$
5. $6827 \times 10 =$

b) **Divide these numbers by 10 or 100:**

1. $6030 \div 10 =$
2. $8000 \div 100 =$
3. $2550 \div 10 =$
4. $9800 \div 100 =$
5. $4600 \div 100 =$

c) **Now try these:**

1. $5864 \times 10 =$
2. $3600 \div 100 =$
3. $452 \times 100 =$
4. $4590 \div 10 =$
5. $8800 \div 100 =$

Gold

a) **Multiply these numbers by 10 or 100:**

1. $23356 \times 10 =$
2. $6854 \times 100 =$
3. $34235 \times 10 =$
4. $74054 \times 100 =$
5. $18279 \times 100 =$

b) **Divide these numbers by 10 or 100:**

1. $75890 \div 10 =$
2. $60900 \div 100 =$
3. $45870 \div 10 =$
4. $55600 \div 100 =$
5. $16500 \div 100 =$

c) **Now try these:**

1. $16493 \times 1000 =$
2. $362000 \div 1000 =$
3. $20348 \times 1000 =$
4. $98000 \div 1000 =$
5. $429000 \times 1000 =$

 **Training Tips**

 To multiply by 100 move the digits two places to the left.

 To divide by 100 move the digits two places to the right.

Ordering numbers

> means **greater than** e.g. 587 > 203   < means **less than** e.g. 105 < 203

= means **equal to** e.g. 3 × 4 = 12

Bronze

a) Complete these number sentences using >, < or =

1. 624 ☐ 423
2. 358 ☐ 894
3. 6 + 6 ☐ 12
4. 765 ☐ 703
5. 5 + 5 ☐ 84

b) Order these numbers from smallest to largest:

1. 326   428   328   625
2. 587   642   578   907
3. 152   987   234   304
4. 783   726   894   956
5. 343   767   654   845

c) Give two numbers between the following:

1. 26 ⌐⌐⌐ 30
2. 35 ⌐⌐⌐⌐⌐ 42
3. 64 ⌐⌐⌐⌐⌐ 70
4. 28 ⌐⌐⌐⌐⌐⌐⌐⌐⌐ 38
5. 79 ⌐⌐⌐⌐⌐⌐⌐⌐⌐ 89

Silver

a) Complete these number sentences using >, < or =

1. 4037 ☐ 3965
2. 9865 ☐ 12 345
3. 4 × 5 ☐ 35
4. 5 × 6 ☐ 30
5. 7976 ☐ 7954

b) Order these numbers from smallest to largest:

1. 2098   428
   2983   10 987
2. 96 328   5284
   5428   3202
3. 84 512   65 457
   23 421   30 751
4. 5831   42 126
   89 414   94 752
5. 87 421   81 235
   84 215   86 321

c) Give three numbers between the following:

1. 1006   1011
2. 6585   6590
3. 6124   6128
4. 8457   8462
5. 6312   6322

Gold

a) Complete these number sentences using >, < or =

1. 6 × 6 ☐ 5 × 8
2. 10 ÷ 15 ☐ 5 × 5
3. 4 × 8 ☐ 5 × 3
4. 9 × 3 ☐ 10 × 3
5. 8 × 6 ☐ 20 ÷ 14

b) Order these numbers from smallest to largest:

1. 2 025 710   1 024 532
   4 024 451   7 034 741
2. 2 015 412   6 420 140
   5 780 120   1 050 907
3. 5 849 304   1 234 345
   4 356 354   4 612 315
4. 2 104 512   4 102 014
   2 510 351   2 641 205
5. 1 025 410   1 024 512
   1 028 451   1 036 541

c) Give the number halfway between the following two numbers:

1. 26   30   2. 350   354
3. 645   649   4. 28   38
5. 79   89

Training Tips

 Look at the value of each digit to help.

 Make sure you know what each of the symbols means.

Estimating

Estimating is a very useful skill. You need to be able to estimate a number on a number line.

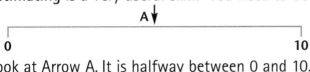

Look at Arrow A. It is halfway between 0 and 10. The number halfway between 0 and 10 is 5 so Arrow A must be pointing to 5.

Look at Arrow B. It is more that halfway and it is very close to 10.

I estimate it is pointing to 9.

Bronze

a) Estimate the numbers that these arrows are pointing to:

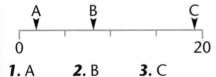

1. A   **2.** B   **3.** C

b) Estimate the numbers that these arrows are pointing to:

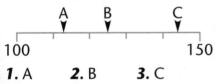

1. A   **2.** B   **3.** C

c) Estimate how many A4 sheets of paper you would need to cover the following:

1. Your table

2. The classroom whiteboard

3. The classroom floor

Silver

a) Estimate the numbers that these arrows are pointing to:

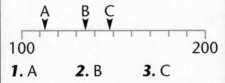

1. A   **2.** B   **3.** C

b) Estimate the numbers that these arrows are pointing to:

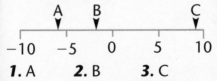

1. A   **2.** B   **3.** C

c) Estimate the length in cm of the following items:

1. Your maths book

2. Your table

3. Your classroom door

Gold

a) Estimate the numbers that these arrows are pointing to:

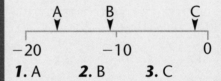

1. A   **2.** B   **3.** C

b) Estimate the numbers that these arrows are pointing to:

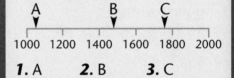

1. A   **2.** B   **3.** C

c) Estimate the following answers:

1. How many days have you been alive?

2. How many hairs are on your head?

3. How many paper clips would fit in a cup?

Training Tips

 Use what you already know to help you estimate.

 Imagine a number line when you estimate.

Rounding

Look at this number line. The arrow is pointing to 180.
Which multiple of 100 is it nearest to?

180 rounded to the nearest 100 is 200.

Remember, we always round 5 up
e.g. 15 rounds up to 20

100 110 120 130 140 150 160 170 180 190 **200**

Bronze

a) **Round these numbers to the nearest 10 using the number line below to help you:**

0   10   20   30

1. 19   **2.** 26   **3.** 23

4. 15   **5.** 8

b) **Now try these without a number line (remember, you can always draw your own!):**

1. 49   **2.** 86   **3.** 72

4. 65   **5.** 51

c) **Round these numbers to the nearest 100 using the number line below to help you:**

0   100   200   300   400   500

1. 289   **2.** 324   **3.** 496

4. 35   **5.** 142

Silver

a) **Round these numbers to the nearest 10:**

1. 163
2. 278
3. 631
4. 465
5. 1324

b) **Round these numbers to the nearest 100:**

1. 862
2. 943
3. 210
4. 750
5. 1874

c) **Round these numbers to the nearest 1000:**

1. 1623
2. 3429
3. 2934
4. 1500
5. 6299

Gold

a) **Round these numbers to the nearest 10:**

1. 5127
2. 2154
3. 8555
4. 6549
5. 96213

b) **Round these numbers to the nearest 100:**

1. 8623
2. 3452
3. 2569
4. 6250
5. 89483

c) **Round these numbers to the nearest 1000:**

1. 85512
2. 42135
3. 67712
4. 81500
5. 62895

Training Tips

Less than 5 – round down
5 or more – round up

Draw number lines to help you.

Negative numbers

Numbers less than zero are called **negative numbers**.
You find negative numbers in temperatures.
−6°C is very cold!
To read these numbers we use the word **negative**
or **minus**.

−8 is read as minus 8 or negative 8.

A number line can help when we add and
subtract negative numbers.

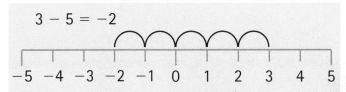

$$3 - 5 = -2$$

| −5 | −4 | −3 | −2 | −1 | 0 | 1 | 2 | 3 | 4 | 5 |

Bronze

a) Write number lines into
   your book and fill in the
   missing numbers:

1. −5, ☐, ☐, −2, −1, 0, 1
      ☐, 3, 4

2. ☐, −6, ☐, −2, 0, 2, 4,
      ☐, 8, ☐

3. −50, ☐, ☐, −20, −10,
      ☐, 10, ☐

4. −15, ☐, −5, ☐, 5, ☐,
      ☐, 20

5. ☐, −9, ☐, −3, ☐, 3, 6,
      ☐, ☐

b) Use a number line to
   order these numbers,
   smallest to largest:

1. 2, −4, −1, 8, 0

2. −8, 6 −2, −4, 9

3. 4, −4, 11, 6, 10

4. −3, −7, 5, −11, 2

5. −12, 8, −3, 4, 0

Silver

a) Finish these sequences:

1. 4, 2, 0, −2, ☐, ☐, ☐, ☐

2. 8, 4, 0, −4, ☐, ☐, ☐, ☐

3. 10, 5, 0, ☐, ☐, ☐, ☐

4. 6, 3, ☐, ☐, ☐, ☐, ☐

5. 12, 6, ☐, ☐, ☐, ☐, ☐

b) Use the thermometer
   to help you work
   out the new
   temperature:

1. 4° − 6° = ☐°

2. 2° − 8° = ☐°

3. −5° + 7° = ☐°

4. −9° + 6° = ☐°

5. 1° − 8° = ☐°

Gold

a) Order these numbers,
   smallest to largest:

1. −6, −180, −132, −200, 8

2. −600, −11, 8, 64, 0

3. −33, 30, −32, 0, −30

4. −6, −66, −666, 6, 66

5. −1123, −345, −5643, −3,
      −927

b) Answer these sums:

1. 12 − 30 =

2. 52 − 102 =

3. −36 + 48 =

4. −99 + 112 =

5. −881 + 882 =

c) Work out these
   temperature word
   problems:

1. The temperature is 15°C.
      It drops 34°C. What is the
      new temperature?

2. The temperature is −8°C.
      It rises 12°C. What is the
      new temperature?

**Training
Tips**

**Negative numbers are less
than zero.**

**Make sure you remember to
use the minus sign if the
number is below zero.**

Sequences

A **sequence** is a list of numbers that are connected by a pattern or rule.

This is a sequence: | 2, 4, 6, 8, 10, ... The **rule** for this sequence is +2.

To help you find the rule for a sequence, look at the gaps between the numbers.

For the sequence above, the gap between each number is two.

Bronze

Using the rule given, write the next five numbers in each sequence:

1. +5   1, 6, ...
2. +10   6, 16, ...
3. −2   20, 18, ...
4. −10   70, 60, ...
5. +3   15, 18, ...
6. −4   40, 36, ...
7. −20   120, 100, ...
8. +100 36, 136, ...
9. +100 9, 109, ...
10. +100 25, 125, ...
11. +9   11, 20, ...
12. +11   0, 11, ...
13. −6   50, 44, ...
14. +7   9, 16, ...
15. −3   26, 23, ...

Silver

a) Using the rule given, write the next five numbers in each sequence:

1. +6   11, 17, ...
2. +9   112, 121, ...
3. −10   334, 324, ...
4. +11   264, 275, ...
5. −100 1426, 1326, ...

b) Copy and complete these sequences. Write a sentence to describe the rule.

1. 16, 18, ☐, ☐, ☐, ☐
2. 6, 12, ☐, ☐, ☐, ☐
3. ☐, ☐, 20, 25, 30, ☐, ☐
4. 8, 18, 28, ☐, ☐, ☐, ☐
5. ☐, 19, ☐, 39, 49, ☐, 69, ☐
6. ☐, ☐, 69, 59, 49, ☐, ☐
7. 116, 120, 124, ☐, ☐, ☐, ☐, ☐

Gold

Copy and complete these sequences. Write down the rule for each.

1. ☐, 19, ☐, 39, 49, ☐, 69, ☐, ☐
2. 1, 4, 9, ☐, 25, ☐, ☐, ☐, ☐
3. 315, ☐, ☐, ☐, ☐, 365, ☐
4. ☐, 67, ☐, 167, ☐, ☐, 317, ☐
5. 2, 7, 12, 17, ☐, ☐, ☐, ☐, ☐
6. 6, 4, 2, ☐, ☐, ☐, ☐,
7. 0.2, 0.4, 0.6, ☐, ☐, ☐, ☐, ☐
8. ☐, 1.2, 1.5, 1.8, ☐, ☐, ☐, ☐
9. ☐, 0.03, 0.04, 0.05, ☐, ☐, ☐, ☐
10. 15, 12, 9, ☐, ☐, ☐, ☐, ☐

Training Tips

Look at the difference between numbers to help you find the rule.

Use commas to separate the numbers in a sequence.

Odd and even numbers

Even numbers
Even numbers can be divided by 2 exactly.
They end in either 0, 2, 4, 6 or 8.
Even   26, 34, 72, 148, 62450

Odd numbers
Odd numbers cannot be divided by 2 exactly.
They end in either 1, 3, 5, 7 or 9.
Odd   35, 87, 99, 131, 75645

Bronze

a) Decide whether these numbers are odd or even:
1. 35
2. 68
3. 24
4. 157

b) Add these pairs of even numbers:
1. 8 + 6 =
2. 14 + 2 =
3. 10 + 8 =
4. 12 + 20 =
5. What do you notice about the answers? Are they all odd or even?

c) Add these pairs of odd numbers:
1. 9 + 9 =
2. 7 + 5 =
3. 13 + 3 =
4. 11 + 7 =
5. What do you notice about the answers? Are they all odd or even?

Silver

a) Answer these sums and decide whether the answer is odd or even:
1. 26 + 12 =
2. 34 + 24 =
3. 4 × 5 =
4. 3 × 6 =

b) Add these sets of three even numbers:
1. 14 + 12 + 6 =
2. 30 + 26 + 4 =
3. 2 + 40 + 18 =
4. 8 + 16 + 8 =
5. Are all the answers odd or even? Write your answer as a rule.

c) Add these sets of three odd numbers:
1. 11 + 13 + 9 =
2. 25 + 7 + 5 =
3. 53 + 9 + 7 =
4. 17 + 7 + 3 =
5. Are all the answers odd or even? Write your answer as a rule.

Gold

a) Answer these sums and decide whether the answer is odd or even:
1. 15 + 12 − 5 =
2. 25 + 36 − 12 =
3. 8 × 6 =
4. 9 × 5 =

b) Investigate these patterns in adding odd and even numbers:
1. 36 + 12 =
Investigate adding three more pairs of even numbers.
2. Complete this rule: even number + even number = ...
3. 47 + 13 =
Investigate adding three more pairs of odd numbers.
4. Complete this rule: Odd number + odd number = ...
5. Investigate what happens when you add an odd number and an even number. What is the rule?

Training Tips

 Even numbers are in your 2 times table.

 Look at the last digit of the number to tell if it is even or odd.

Multiples

A multiple is the result of multiplying one number by another.

Example
All the answers in the 4 times table are multiples of 4.
4, 8, 12, 16, 20, 24, 28, 32, 36, 40

 Bronze

 Silver

 **Gold**

Bronze

a) Write down the first four multiples of the following times tables:

1. 2   *2.* 3   *3.* 4
4. 5   *5.* 10

b) Write true or false next to these statements:

1. 6 is a multiple 2
2. 40 is a multiple of 10
3. 12 is a multiple of 5
4. 25 is a multiple of 2
5. 15 is a multiple of 3

c) Find the odd one out:

1. 3, 9, 12, 2
2. 5, 10, 12, 15
3. 30, 60, 20, 15
4. 3, 8, 10, 20
5. 30, 60, 100, 800

Silver

a) Write down the first six multiples of the following times tables:

1. 4   *2.* 6   *3.* 7
4. 8   *5.* 9

b) Write true or false next to these statements:

1. 28 is a multiple of 4
2. 36 is a multiple of 6
3. 46 is a multiple of 7
4. 72 is a multiple of 8
5. 71 is a multiple of 9

c) Find the odd one out:

1. 21, 12, 33, 5
2. 28, 55, 70, 14
3. 16, 80, 11, 40
4. 36, 72, 81, 98
5. 36, 53, 66, 72

Gold

a) Write down the first six multiples of the following times tables:

1. 11   *2.* 7   *3.* 15
4. 8   *5.* 25

b) Write true or false next to these statements:

1. 92 is a multiple of 4
2. 95 is a multiple of 8
3. 111 is a multiple of 11
4. 60 is a multiple of 15
5. 165 is a multiple of 55

c) Find two numbers that are multiples of:

1. 3 and 2
2. 10 and 4
3. 5 and 3
4. 4 and 3
5. 7 and 5

 **Training Tips**

 Multiples are the numbers in your times tables.

 Use a multiplication square to help you.

Square numbers

When you multiply a number by itself, the answer is called a **square number.**

Example
3 × 3 = 9 so three squared = 9

They are called square numbers because they can be represented by dots in the form of a square.

A simple way to write the square of 3 is 3^2

The square of 3 is 3 × 3 = 9.
9 dots can form a square

The square of 5 is 5 × 5 = 25.
25 dots can form a square.

Bronze

a) **Work out the following answers using the drawings to help you:**

1. 2 × 2 =   **2.** 3 × 3 =

3. 4 × 4 =   **4.** 5 × 5 =

5. 6 × 6 =

b) **Are these square numbers? Yes or no? Try to draw them as pictures – can they make a square?**

1. 4   **2.** 6   **3.** 14

4. 9   **5.** 36

c) **One number in each list is a square number. Which one?**

1. 14, 16, 18

2. 20, 25, 30

3. 0, 1, 3

4. 8, 4, 6

5. 11, 36, 29

Silver

a) **Work out the following square numbers:**

1. $2^2 = 2 \times 2 =$

2. $3^2 = 3 \times 3 =$

3. $4^2 = 4 \times 4 =$

4. $5^2 = 5 \times 5 =$

5. $6^2 = 6 \times 6 =$

b) **Are these square numbers? Yes or no? Try to draw them as pictures – can they make a square?**

1. 10   **2.** 27   **3.** 25

4. 42   **5.** 80

c) **One number in each list is a square number. Which one?**

1. 4, 8, 18, 12, 24

2. 32, 60, 46, 64, 23

3. 65, 25, 10, 45, 50

4. 44, 24, 4, 34, 84

5. 6, 56, 36, 26, 96

Gold

a) **Work out the following:**

1. 5^2 **2.** 6^2 **3.** 7^2

4. 8^2 **5.** 9^2

b) **One number in each list is a square number. Which one?**

1. 29, 99, 90, 9, 89

2. 21, 7, 31, 14, 1

3. 83, 8, 81, 80, 88

4. 45, 49, 40, 44, 41

5. 130, 200, 144, 140, 104

Training Tips

 A square number is a number multiplied by itself.

 If you see 3^2 remember it means 3 x 3.

Factors

A **factor** is a number that divides exactly into another number.

Example
$3 \times 5 = 15$ so 3 and 5 are both factors of 15

We list factors like this
Factors of 10: 1, 2, 5, 10

You can also look at the highest factor that two numbers share.
The highest factor shared by 10 and 15 is 5.

Bronze

a) **For which number are these the pairs of factors?**

1. 1×6, 2×3

2. 1×11

3. 1×9, 3×3

4. 1×14, 2×7

5. 1×12, 2×6, 3×4

b) **Complete these pairs of factors:**

1. 25: 1×25, $5 \times \square$

2. 27: $1 \times \square$, 3×9

3. 12: 1×12, $2 \times \square$, 3×4

4. 35: 1×35, $5 \times \square$

5. 20: 1×20, $2 \times \square$, 4×5

c) **Write the missing factors:**

1. Factors of 12:
   1 2 $\square$ 4 6 12

2. Factors of 8:
   1 2 $\square$ 8

3. Factors of 4:
   $\square$ 2 4

4. Factors of 15:
   1 3 $\square$ 15

Silver

a) **For which number are these the pairs of factors?**

1. 1×37

2. 1×15, 3×5

3. 1×46, 2×23

4. 1×33, 3×11

5. 1×54, 2×27, 6×9

b) **Write all the pairs of factors for each number:**

1. 10   *2.* 4   *3.* 16

4. 24   *5.* 32

c) **List all of the factors of these numbers:**

1. 6   *2.* 14   *3.* 26

4. 18   *5.* 16

Gold

a) **Write the missing factors:**

1. Factors of 28:
   1 2 $\square$ $\square$ 14 28

2. Factors of 32:
   1 2 $\square$ $\square$ 16 32

3. Factors of 34:
   1 $\square$ 17 $\square$

4. Factors of 45:
   1 3 $\square$ 9 15 $\square$

5. Factors of 24:
   1 2 $\square$ 4 6 $\square$ 12 24

b) **List all the factors of these numbers:**

1. 40   *2.* 54   *3.* 13

4. 60   *5.* 100

c) **Write the highest factor common to these numbers:**

1. 25 and 35

2. 12 and 16

3. 14 and 21

4. 18 and 30

5. 10 and 20

Training Tips

Think of factors as pairs of numbers whose product is the target number.

Work methodically to find factors – does 2 divide into the number 3?

Writing fractions

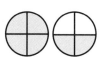

1. A fraction is a part of something. Each fraction is set out like this:

Numerator $\longrightarrow \dfrac{1}{3}$
Denominator $\longrightarrow$

2. When the numerator is larger than the denominator, like $\frac{6}{4}$, we call this an **improper fraction**.

3. A third ($\frac{1}{3}$) of this circle is coloured. 1 part of 3.

$\frac{6}{4}$ is coloured or 1 whole and $\frac{2}{4} = 1\frac{2}{4}$

4. $1\frac{2}{4}$ is called a **mixed number**. It is a whole number plus a fraction.

Bronze

a) **What fraction is shaded?**

1.   2.

3.   4.

b) **Write these fractions:**

1. One half
2. One quarter
3. One fifth
4. One third
5. Two sixths

c) **Write these numbers as mixed numbers and improper fractions:**

1.  $= \dfrac{\square}{4} = 1\dfrac{\square}{4}$

2.  $= \dfrac{\square}{4} = 2\dfrac{\square}{4}$

Silver

a) **Write the following fractions:**

1. Numerator = 2
   Denominator = 6
2. Numerator = 3
   Denominator = 4
3. Three fifths
4. Five eighths

b) **What fraction is shaded? Write as a mixed number and improper fraction**

1.

2.

c) **Copy and complete the following:**

1. $\frac{6}{4} = 1\frac{\square}{4}$ 2. $\frac{10}{3} = 3\frac{\square}{3}$

3. $\frac{\square}{2} = 2\frac{1}{\square}$ 4. $\frac{\square}{4} = 1\frac{3}{\square}$

Gold

a) **Write these fractions:**

1. Numerator = 11
   Denominator = 27
2. Numerator = 16
   Denominator = 34
3. Twenty elevenths
4. Sixteen twentieths

b) **Change the following to improper fractions:**

1. $11\frac{3}{4}$ 2. $6\frac{4}{8}$
3. $7\frac{2}{9}$ 4. $11\frac{2}{3}$
5. $10\frac{2}{5}$

c) **Change to mixed numbers:**

1. $\frac{16}{5}$ 2. $\frac{11}{2}$
3. $\frac{25}{3}$ 4. $\frac{19}{6}$
5. $\frac{100}{20}$

Training Tips

Make sure you know which is the numerator and which is the denominator.

Practise changing an improper fraction to a mixed number and vice versa.

Fractions of amounts

$\frac{1}{4}$ of 16 is the same as 16 ÷ 4 = 4

Example
What is $\frac{1}{5}$ of £25?

25 ÷ 5 = 5 so $\frac{1}{5}$ of £25 = £5

Bronze

a) Find $\frac{1}{2}$ of:

1. 8

2. 20

3. 16

4. 30

5. 18

b) Find $\frac{1}{10}$ of:

1. 20

2. 80

3. 10

4. 100

5. 70

c) Find $\frac{1}{5}$ of:

1. 45

2. 25

3. 50

4. 30

5. 55

Silver

a) Find:

1. $\frac{1}{10}$ of 80

2. $\frac{1}{5}$ of 45

3. $\frac{1}{8}$ of 16

4. $\frac{1}{4}$ of 32

5. $\frac{1}{9}$ of 81

b) Complete:

1. $\frac{1}{5}$ of 20 = 4 $\frac{2}{5}$ of 20 = ☐

2. $\frac{1}{4}$ of 12 = ☐ $\frac{2}{4}$ of 12 = ☐

3. $\frac{1}{10}$ of 60 = ☐ $\frac{3}{10}$ of 60 = ☐

4. $\frac{1}{10}$ of 50p = ☐ $\frac{4}{10}$ of 50p = ☐

5. $\frac{1}{9}$ of 45p = ☐ $\frac{6}{9}$ of 45p = ☐

c) Find:

1. $\frac{2}{3}$ of 75p

2. $\frac{3}{5}$ of 25 m

3. $\frac{6}{8}$ of £56

4. $\frac{2}{9}$ of 72 cm

5. $\frac{1}{10}$ of £1

Gold

a) Complete:

1. $\frac{1}{10}$ of 80 = ☐
    $\frac{6}{10}$ of 80 = ☐

2. $\frac{1}{7}$ of 35 = ☐
    $\frac{5}{7}$ of 35 = ☐

3. $\frac{1}{8}$ of 24 = ☐
    $\frac{3}{8}$ of 24 = ☐

4. $\frac{1}{6}$ of 54 = ☐
    $\frac{4}{6}$ of 54 = ☐

5. $\frac{1}{9}$ of 81 = ☐
    $\frac{7}{9}$ of 81 = ☐

b) Find:

1. $\frac{4}{6}$ of 30

2. $\frac{5}{8}$ of 56

3. $\frac{9}{11}$ of 110

4. $\frac{6}{7}$ of 84

5. $\frac{14}{25}$ of 250

c) Find:

1. $\frac{7}{10}$ of 120cm

2. $\frac{2}{5}$ of 1 litre

3. $\frac{6}{10}$ of 1m

4. $\frac{311}{1000}$ of 1kg

5. $\frac{69}{100}$ of £1

Training Tips

 Divide by the denominator.

 Multiply by the numerator.

Equivalent fractions

Looking at these diagrams you can see that the same area is shaded. So if $\frac{1}{4}$ is coloured, it is the same as $\frac{2}{8}$. We say $\frac{1}{4}$ is equivalent to $\frac{2}{8}$.

   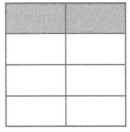

$\frac{1}{4}$ $\frac{2}{8}$

You can make equivalent fractions by multiplying or dividing the numerator and denominator by the same number.

Multiplying

$$\frac{1}{4} \begin{smallmatrix}(\times 2)\\(\times 2)\end{smallmatrix} = \frac{2}{8} \begin{smallmatrix}(\times 2)\\(\times 2)\end{smallmatrix} = \frac{4}{16}$$

Dividing

$$\frac{9}{27} \begin{smallmatrix}(\div 3)\\(\div 3)\end{smallmatrix} = \frac{3}{9} \begin{smallmatrix}(\div 3)\\(\div 3)\end{smallmatrix} = \frac{1}{3}$$

All these fractions are equivalent.

Bronze

a) Complete the following fractions:

1. $\frac{1}{2} \begin{smallmatrix}(\times 2)\\(\times 2)\end{smallmatrix} = \frac{}{4}$

2. $\frac{1}{3} \begin{smallmatrix}(\times 2)\\(\times 2)\end{smallmatrix} = \frac{}{6}$

3. $\frac{3}{5} \begin{smallmatrix}(\times 3)\\(\times 3)\end{smallmatrix} = \frac{}{15}$

4. $\frac{2}{4} \begin{smallmatrix}(\div 2)\\(\div 2)\end{smallmatrix} = \frac{}{2}$

5. $\frac{6}{8} \begin{smallmatrix}(\div 2)\\(\div 2)\end{smallmatrix} = \frac{}{4}$

b) Match the fractions to their equivalents:

1. $\frac{1}{2}$ $\frac{5}{15}$

2. $\frac{1}{6}$ $\frac{2}{10}$

3. $\frac{1}{4}$ $\frac{3}{6}$

4. $\frac{1}{3}$ $\frac{3}{12}$

5. $\frac{1}{5}$ $\frac{3}{18}$

Silver

a) Complete:

1. $\frac{2}{6} \begin{smallmatrix}(\times 3)\\(\times 3)\end{smallmatrix} = \frac{}{18}$

2. $\frac{4}{5} \begin{smallmatrix}(\times 4)\\(\times 4)\end{smallmatrix} = \frac{}{20}$

3. $\frac{2}{3} \begin{smallmatrix}(\times 6)\\(\times 6)\end{smallmatrix} = \frac{}{18}$

4. $\frac{2}{4} \begin{smallmatrix}(\times 5)\\(\times 5)\end{smallmatrix} = \frac{}{}$

5. $\frac{7}{10} \begin{smallmatrix}(\times 10)\\(\times 10)\end{smallmatrix} = \frac{}{}$

b) Match the fractions to their equivalents:

1. $\frac{3}{4}$ $\frac{33}{36}$

2. $\frac{4}{5}$ $\frac{60}{100}$

3. $\frac{8}{10}$ $\frac{9}{12}$

4. $\frac{11}{12}$ $\frac{36}{45}$

5. $\frac{6}{10}$ $\frac{80}{100}$

Gold

a) Complete the following:

1. $\frac{6}{10} = \frac{}{100}$

2. $\frac{11}{13} = \frac{22}{}$

3. $\frac{9}{15} = \frac{}{30}$

4. $\frac{7}{10} = \frac{}{1000}$

5. $\frac{4}{5} = \frac{36}{}$

b) Match the fractions to their equivalents:

1. $\frac{10}{14}$ $\frac{36}{81}$

2. $\frac{6}{10}$ $\frac{49}{56}$

3. $\frac{4}{9}$ $\frac{20}{28}$

4. $\frac{7}{8}$ $\frac{30}{42}$

5. $\frac{5}{7}$ $\frac{600}{1000}$

 **Training Tips**

 Multiply or divide the numerator and denominator by the same number.

 Fractions where the numerator and denominator are the same = 1.

Ordering fractions

$\frac{1}{2}$ $\frac{1}{4}$ $\frac{1}{8}$

Look at these fractions. It is hard to order them because the denominators are different.
We need the denominators to be the same by making them equivalent.

$\frac{1}{2} = \frac{4}{8}$ $\frac{1}{4} = \frac{2}{8}$ $\frac{1}{8} = \frac{1}{8}$

Now we can order them.

$\frac{1}{8}$ $\frac{2}{8}$ $\frac{4}{8}$

We can also place them on a number line

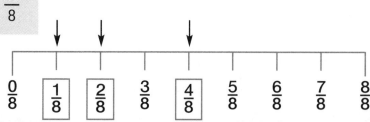

Bronze

a) Order these:

1. $\frac{6}{8}$ $\frac{2}{8}$ $\frac{1}{8}$

2. $\frac{9}{10}$ $\frac{3}{10}$ $\frac{7}{10}$

3. $\frac{2}{5}$ $\frac{1}{5}$ $\frac{3}{5}$

4. $\frac{7}{8}$ $\frac{3}{8}$ $\frac{5}{8}$

5. $\frac{26}{100}$ $\frac{89}{100}$ $\frac{35}{100}$

b) Which is the largest?

1. $\frac{1}{2}$ or $\frac{1}{4}$ 2. $\frac{2}{3}$ or $\frac{1}{2}$

3. $\frac{4}{4}$ or $\frac{11}{12}$ 4. $\frac{1}{3}$ or $\frac{1}{5}$

c) Place the following fractions on your number line:

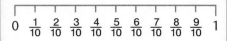

1. $\frac{2}{10}$ 2. $\frac{1}{2}$

3. $\frac{8}{10}$ 4. $\frac{60}{100}$

Silver

a) Order these:

1. $\frac{1}{2}$ $\frac{3}{8}$ $\frac{2}{2}$

2. $\frac{4}{5}$ $\frac{2}{10}$ $\frac{3}{10}$

3. $\frac{1}{3}$ $\frac{2}{3}$ $\frac{5}{6}$

4. $\frac{9}{10}$ $\frac{23}{100}$ $\frac{4}{10}$

5. $\frac{6}{20}$ $\frac{4}{10}$ $\frac{8}{20}$

b) Which is bigger?

1. $\frac{6}{10}$ or $\frac{4}{5}$ 2. $\frac{12}{13}$ or $\frac{2}{2}$

3. $\frac{2}{8}$ or $\frac{6}{16}$ 4. $\frac{6}{11}$ or $\frac{2}{88}$

c) Place the following fractions on your number line:

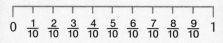

1. $\frac{2}{10}$ 2. $\frac{4}{10}$

3. $\frac{1}{5}$ 4. $\frac{4}{5}$

Gold

a) Order these:

1. $\frac{1}{4}$ $\frac{1}{2}$ $\frac{6}{8}$

2. $\frac{4}{6}$ $\frac{1}{3}$ $\frac{1}{2}$

3. $\frac{2}{10}$ $\frac{4}{5}$ $\frac{1}{2}$

4. $\frac{2}{4}$ $\frac{3}{3}$ $\frac{2}{6}$

5. $\frac{1}{2}$ $\frac{2}{3}$ $\frac{3}{4}$

b) Which is bigger?

1. $\frac{2}{3}$ or $\frac{4}{5}$ 2. $\frac{1}{6}$ or $\frac{3}{4}$

3. $\frac{10}{12}$ or $\frac{3}{5}$ 4. $\frac{6}{8}$ or $\frac{16}{24}$

c) Place the following fractions on your number line:

1. $\frac{5}{10}$ 2. $\frac{3}{10}$

3. $\frac{6}{20}$ 4. $\frac{3}{5}$

Training Tips

 Change each fraction to the same denominator to order them.

 Look at the number line carefully and find what each division means.

Fractions and decimals

Every fraction can be expressed as a decimal.

We already know

$\frac{1}{10} = 0.1$ $\frac{3}{10} = 0.3$ $\frac{1}{100} = 0.01$ $\frac{7}{100} = 0.07$

Other fractions also have equivalent decimals.

$\frac{1}{2} = 0.5$ $\frac{1}{4} = 0.25$ $\frac{1}{5} = 0.2$

Bronze

a) Match each fraction with a decimal:

1. $\frac{1}{4}$ 0.6
2. $\frac{2}{10}$ 0.4
3. $\frac{1}{2}$ 0.2
4. $\frac{6}{10}$ 0.25
5. $\frac{4}{10}$ 0.5

b) Write these as a decimal:

1. $\frac{3}{10}$
2. $\frac{7}{10}$
3. $\frac{5}{10}$
4. $\frac{9}{10}$
5. $\frac{1}{5}$

c) Write these as a fraction:

1. 0.6
2. 0.2
3. 0.8
4. 0.5
5. 0.1

Silver

a) Match each fraction with a decimal:

1. $\frac{2}{5}$ 0.19
2. $\frac{8}{100}$ 0.5
3. $\frac{3}{4}$ 0.4
4. $\frac{19}{100}$ 0.75
5. $\frac{1}{2}$ 0.08

b) Write these as a decimal:

1. $\frac{98}{100}$
2. $\frac{73}{100}$
3. $\frac{46}{100}$
4. $\frac{4}{100}$
5. $\frac{3}{5}$

c) Write these as a fraction:

1. 0.24
2. 0.39
3. 0.04
4. 0.25
5. 0.63

Gold

a) Match each fraction with a decimal:

1. $\frac{4}{5}$ 0.27
2. $\frac{5}{1000}$ 0.75
3. $\frac{6}{100}$ 0.8
4. $\frac{3}{4}$ 0.005
5. $\frac{27}{100}$ 0.06

b) Write these as a decimal:

1. $2\frac{23}{100}$
2. $\frac{523}{100}$
3. $\frac{167}{100}$
4. $\frac{8654}{1000}$
5. $\frac{2375}{100}$

c) Write these as a fraction:

1. 1.76
2. 8.34
3. 8.23
4. 46.75
5. 36.78

 Training Tips

 Learn these:
- $\frac{1}{2} = 0.5$ • $\frac{1}{4} = 0.25$
- $\frac{1}{5} = 0.2$

 Change fractions into tenths and hundredths so you can write them as decimals.

Decimal fractions

Decimals are another way of writing fractions.

The fraction $\frac{13}{100}$ can be written as 0.13.

The 1 equals $\frac{10}{100}$ and the 3 equals $\frac{3}{100}$.

Look at this table for 3.675:

3	. 6	7	5
3 units	. 6 tenths	7 hundredths	5 thousandths
3 units	. $\frac{6}{10}$	$\frac{7}{100}$	$\frac{5}{1000}$

 Bronze

a) Write these decimals in words:

1. 0.2 = Nought point ☐
2. 0.8 = Nought point ☐
3. 6.2 = Six point ☐
4. 3.4 = ☐ point ☐
5. 2.7 = ☐ point ☐

b) Write these numbers in figures:

1. Nought point three
2. Three point four
3. Nine point six
4. Five point six
5. Two point eight

c) Partition these numbers:

1. 8.4 = 8 + ☐
2. 9.2 = ☐ + 0.2
3. 6.7 = 6 + ☐
4. 8.2 = ☐ + ☐
5. 5.3 = ☐ + ☐

Silver

a) Write the decimal fraction that is the same as the following:

1. Three tenths and four hundredths
2. Forty-six tenths and seven hundredths
3. Nine and nine hundredths
4. Twenty-one and five hundredths
5. Twenty-one hundredths

b) What does the digit in blue represent?

1. **6**.25   2. 9.**2**4   3. 1.6**2**
4. **1**.12   5. 7.8**2**

c) Partition these decimals:

1. 7.23 = ☐ + 0.2 + ☐
2. 4.98 = 4 + ☐ + ☐
3. 8.32 = ☐ + ☐ + 0.02
4. 3.62 = ☐ + ☐ + ☐
5. 6.24 = ☐ + ☐ + ☐

Gold

a) Write the decimal fraction that is the same as the following:

1. Three tenths, four hundredths and six thousandths
2. Forty-six tenths, three hundredths and seven thousandths
3. Nine and nine thousandths
4. Twenty-one, five hundredths and three thousandths
5. Thirty-six and seven tenths, nine hundredths and two thousandths

b) What does the digit in blue represent?

1. 6.2**3**5
2. 9.5**2**4
3. 1.96**2**
4. 16.**1**2
5. 7.24**9**

 **Training Tips**

 Read a decimal out loud – 3.6 is 'three point six'.

 Practising with money is a great way to learn about decimals.

Ordering decimals

When ordering decimals, remember to line up each decimal in a column and make sure they have the same number of digits.

Always read numbers from left to right and compare.

Example

Order: 0.42   0.402   0.44
       0.420   0.402   0.440   Answer: 0.402   0.42   0.44

Bronze

0 ————————— 1 ————————— 2

a) Copy the number line. Put each number below on the number line.

1. 1   *2.* 0.5   *3.* 0.9

4. 1.3   *5.* 1.7

b) Which is the largest?

1. 1.9 or 9.2

2. 8.0 or 0.8

3. 6.2 or 62

4. 3.4 or 3.7

5. 18.2 or 1.8

c) Order these decimals, smallest to largest:

1. 6.3, 1.7, 9.7

2. 7.8, 2.4, 4.1

3. 6.2, 8.5, 1.3

4. 9.2, 1.1, 5.0

5. 2.8, 8.2, 6.7

Silver

0.1 ————————— 0.2 ————————— 0.3

a) Copy the number line. Put each number below on the number line.

1. 0.2   *2.* 0.15   *3.* 0.19

4. 0.23   *5.* 0.27

b) Which is bigger?

1. 2.35 or 2.54

2. 3.67 or 36.7

3. 2.89 or 2.73

4. 6.34 or 8.12

5. 9.43 or 9.34

c) Write these measurements in order – smallest to largest:

1. 1.24m, 2.41m, 4.12m, 1.42m

2. 6.69m, 9.66m, 6.66m, 6.99m

3. 2.31m, 1.32m, 2.13m, 1.23m

4. 7.18m, 8.17m, 1.81m, 7.78m

Gold

2.8 ————————— 2.85 ————————— 2.9

a) Copy the number line. Put each number below on the number line.

1. 2.85   *2.* 2.81   *3.* 2.815

4. 2.865   *5.* 2.9

b) Which is bigger?

1. 3.456 or 3.487

2. 87.94 or 8.794

3. 9.532 or 9.542

4. 8.346 or 8.643

5. 11.435 or 11.644

c) Write these decimals in order – smallest first:

1. 8.778, 7.778, 7.787, 8.887

2. 5.664, 6.446, 6.554, 4.455

3. 7.967, 7.667, 7.776, 6.777

4. 1.5, 1.275, 3.75, 1.556

5. 0.112, 0.023, 0.110, 0.00

Training Tips

 If you are ordering numbers with two decimal places, put in the zeros to help.

 To make it easier, place all of the numbers in a column, lining up on the decimal point.

Rounding decimals

Look at this number line. It is divided into tenths. The arrow is pointing to 1.6

| 0 | 0.1 | 0.2 | 0.3 | 0.4 | 0.5 | 0.6 | 0.7 | 0.8 | 0.9 | 1 | 1.1 | 1.2 | 1.3 | 1.4 | 1.5 | 1.6 | 1.7 | 1.8 | 1.9 | 2 | 2.1 | 2.2 | 2.3 | 2.4 | 2.5 | 2.6 | 2.7 | 2.8 | 2.9 | 3 |

We say 1.6 rounded to the nearest whole number is 2.

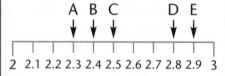 Bronze

a) For each arrow write which number it is pointing to and its nearest whole number.

A B C   D E

| 2 | 2.1 | 2.2 | 2.3 | 2.4 | 2.5 | 2.6 | 2.7 | 2.8 | 2.9 | 3 |

1. A =   **2.** B =   **3.** C =

4. D =   **5.** E =

b) Round these to the nearest whole number:

1. 2.2   **2.** 6.9   **3.** 8.6

4. 7.3   **5.** 3.4

c) Round these to the nearest pound:

1. £3.68

2. £6.41

3. £19.58

4. £47.47

5. £99.09

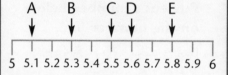 Silver

a) For each arrow write which number it is pointing to and its nearest whole number.

A   B   C D   E

| 5 | 5.1 | 5.2 | 5.3 | 5.4 | 5.5 | 5.6 | 5.7 | 5.8 | 5.9 | 6 |

1. A =   **2.** B =   **3.** C =

4. D =   **5.** E =

b) Round these to the nearest whole number:

1. 2.52   **2.** 6.89   **3.** 8.56

4. 7.35   **5.** 3.42

c) Round these to the nearest ten pence:

1. £3.68

2. £6.41

3. £19.58

4. £47.47

5. £99.09

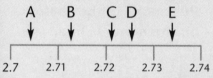 Gold

a) For each arrow write which number it is pointing to and its nearest whole number.

A   B   C D   E

| 2.7 | 2.71 | 2.72 | 2.73 | 2.74 |

1. A =   **2.** B =   **3.** C =

4. D =   **5.** E =

b) Round these to the nearest tenth:

1. 8.814 **2.** 2.845 **3.** 6.062

4. 7.659 **5.** 3.502

c) Round these to the nearest hundredth:

1. 2.342

2. 7.666

3. 0.235

4. 0.474

5. 3.284

Training Tips

 Use number lines to help.

 Read the question carefully so you know what you have to round to.

Percentages of whole numbers

Finding **percentages** of whole numbers is very similar to finding fractions of numbers.

If you are asked to find 10% of 50 then first find the fraction equivalent to 10%, which is $\frac{1}{10}$.

So the question now is to find $\frac{1}{10}$ of 50.

$\frac{1}{10}$ of 50 = 50 ÷ 10 = 5

So 10% of 50 = 5

Once you have found 10% you can find most other percentages by multiplying or dividing.

20% of 50 = 10

Bronze

a) Find 10% of:

1. 60   **2.** 20   **3.** 70

4. 80   **5.** 200

b) Find 50% of:

1. 10   **2.** 8   **3.** 16

4. 22   **5.** 48

c) Find 10% of:

1. 50p   **2.** 90p   **3.** £1

4. £2   **5.** £9

Silver

a) Find 20% of:

1. 40   **2.** 100   **3.** 150

4. 90   **5.** 470

b) Using the number 60:

1. Find 10%

2. Find 20%

3. Find 5%

4. Find 50%

5. Find 80%

c) Work out:

1. 50% of 34

2. 30% of 120

3. 10% of £1.80

4. 40% of £3.20

5. 5% of £6.70

Gold

a) Find 25% of:

1. 20p   **2.** 40p   **3.** £4

4. £12   **5.** £44

b) Find 75% of:

1. 12p   **2.** 24p   **3.** £100

4. £1   **5.** £200

c) Find these amounts:

1. 80% of £1000

2. 20% of 30p

3. 40% of £50

4. 45% of £80

5. 55% of £120

Training Tips

 Make sure you can spell 'percentage'.

 Look for sale signs that offer, for example, 25% off items next time you go shopping.

Percentages

Percentage means the number of parts in 100.

If you look at this grid, 56 squares are coloured.

We say that 56 out of 100 squares are coloured or 56% is coloured.

Every percentage has a decimal and a fraction equivalent.

$56\% = 56$ out of $100 = \frac{56}{100} = 0.56$

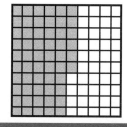

Bronze

a) Look at these grids. Write the percentage that is shaded.

1. 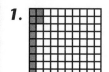 **2.**

3. 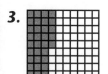 **4.**

b) In your book draw five 10x10 grids of small squares. Shade:

1. 5%   **2.** 26%   **3.** 15%

4. 99%   **5.** 63%

c) Write these percentages as fractions and decimals:

1. $34\% = \frac{}{100} = 0.34$

2. $93\% = \frac{}{100} = \square$

3. $56\% = \frac{}{100} = \square$

4. $72\% = \frac{}{100} = \square$

5. $85\% = \frac{}{100} = \square$

Silver

a) Look at these grids. Write the percentage that is shaded.

1.  **2.**

3. 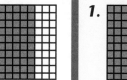 **4.**

b) Write the following percentages as fractions and decimals:

1. 78%   **2.** 39%   **3.** 83%

4. 15%   **5.** 9%

c) Write true or false for the following:

1. $\frac{10}{10} = 10\%$

2. $\frac{3}{4} = 5\%$

3. $0.8 = 80\%$

4. $0.4 = \frac{4}{100}$

5. $0.25 = \frac{1}{4}$

Gold

a) Write each percentage as a fraction and a decimal:

1. 55%   **2.** 7%   **3.** 100%

4. 72%   **5.** 385%

b) Write each fraction as a decimal and a percentage:

1. $\frac{67}{100}$

2. $\frac{1}{2}$

3. $\frac{3}{4}$

4. $\frac{5}{10}$

5. $\frac{1}{5}$

c) Write each decimal as a fraction and a percentage:

1. 0.98

2. 0.05

3. 0.75

4. 0.4

5. 0.7

 **Training Tips**

- 100% is a whole
- $\frac{1}{2} = 50\%$
- $\frac{1}{4} = 25\%$

 Change fractions into hundredths to find percentages.

Ratio and proportion

Ratio is used to make comparisons.

In this pattern for every 1 square there are 2 circles.

If I add another square , I will need to add 2 circles to keep the ratio the same.

We say the ratio of squares to circles is 1:2

Proportion is also used to compare amounts.

For the above picture:

- the proportion of squares is $\frac{1}{3}$
- the proportion of circles is $\frac{2}{3}$

Bronze

Complete the statements:

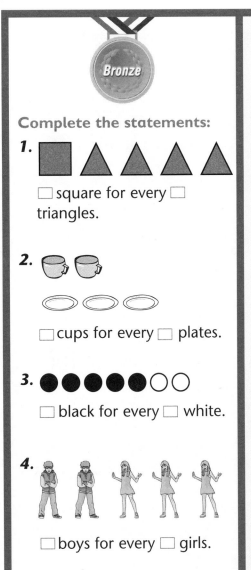

1. ☐ square for every ☐ triangles.

2. ☐ cups for every ☐ plates.

3. ●●●●●○○
   ☐ black for every ☐ white.

4. ☐ boys for every ☐ girls.

Silver

Complete the statements:

1.
   ☐ square for every ☐ triangles.
   ☐ : ☐

2.
   ☐ cups for every ☐ plates.
   ☐ : ☐

3. ●●●
   ○○○○○
   ☐ black for every ☐ white.
   ☐ : ☐

4. ●●●●●●
   ○
   ☐ black for every ☐ white.
   ☐ : ☐

Gold

a) Answer these questions:

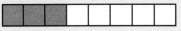

1. What is the ratio of blue to white?

2. What is the proportion of blue?

3. What is the ratio of squares to circles?

4. What is the proportion of circles?

b) For each of these statements write both the ratio and the proportion:

1. 2 circles for every 5 squares

2. 3 triangles for every 4 rectangles

3. 5 circles for every 8 triangles

 **Training Tips**

 You can simplify ratios by dividing each side by the same number.

 When working with ratios, keep both the words and the numbers in the same order.

Recall of addition facts

We all need to learn and practise using addition facts so that we can get quicker in our mental calculations.

 **Bronze**

a) Match the pairs that make 100:

1. 30   60

2. 80   90

3. 40   50

4. 10   20

5. 50   70

b) Match the pairs that make 1000:

1. 300   600

2. 500   200

3. 100   700

4. 400   500

5. 800   900

c) Work out:

1. 20 + 80 =

2. 30 + 70 =

3. 60 + 60 =

4. 80 + 40 =

5. 50 + 90 =

 **Silver**

a) What needs to be added to these decimals to make 1?

1. 0.2   *2.* 0.6   *3.* 0.5

4. 0.7   *5.* 0.1

b) What needs to be added to these numbers to total 100?

1. 67   *2.* 28   *3.* 93

4. 54   *5.* 85

c) What needs to be added to these numbers to total 1000?

1. 650   *2.* 350   *3.* 950

4. 250   *5.* 750

 Gold

a) What needs to be added to these decimals to make 1?

1. 0.54   *2.* 0.26   *3.* 0.72

4. 0.63   *5.* 0.81

b) What needs to be added to these numbers to total 1000?

1. 260   *2.* 830   *3.* 150

4. 680   *5.* 740

c) What needs to be added to these numbers to total 10?

1. 4.6   *2.* 7.2   *3.* 9.4

4. 5.5   *5.* 6.3

 **Training Tips**

 Make sure you know your number bonds to 100.

 Ask a friend how they have remembered them.

Recall of subtraction facts

Addition facts can help you answer subtraction questions.

Example
100 − 30 =
Think about the addition fact you know.

What number goes with 30 to total 100?
Answer: 70

So 100 − 30 = 70

Bronze

a) Work out:
1. 100 − 50 =
2. 100 − 20 =
3. 100 − 90 =
4. 100 − 0 =
5. 100 − 30 =

b) Complete:
1. 100 − ☐ = 60
2. 100 − ☐ = 10
3. 100 − ☐ = 100
4. 100 − ☐ = 40
5. 100 − ☐ = 20

c) Work out:
1. 1000 − 400 =
2. 1000 − 600=
3. 1000 − 200 =
4. 1000 − 800 =
5. 1000 − 100 =

Silver

a) Work out:
1. 1 − 0.8 =
2. 1 − 0.4 =
3. 1 − 0.5 =
4. 1 − 0.9 =
5. 1 − 0.2 =

b) What needs to be subtracted from 100 to make these answers?
1. 62
2. 93
3. 27
4. 56
5. 72

c) Copy and complete:
1. 1000 − ☐ = 950
2. 1000 − ☐ = 750
3. 1000 − ☐ = 250
4. 1000 − ☐ = 450
5. 1000 − ☐ = 850

Gold

a) Work out:
1. 1 − 0.34 =
2. 1 − 0.63 =
3. 1 − 0.86 =
4. 1 − 0.92 =
5. 1 − 0.49 =

b) What needs to be subtracted from 1000 to make these answers?
1. 130
2. 970
3. 250
4. 840
5. 730

c) Copy and complete:
1. 10 − ☐ = 5.6
2. 10 − ☐ = 9.8
3. 10 − ☐ = 3.6
4. 10 − ☐ = 5.7
5. 10 − ☐ = 2.5

Training Tips

 Use your addition facts to help you.

Remember, subtraction is the opposite of addition.

Mental calculations

To solve these sums you are going to use the following two methods.

Method 1

Counting up through the next multiple

We use this method to find differences. Start with the smaller number and count up to the biggest number in the sum. This tells you the difference between them. It is helpful to make jumps to the next 10, then the next 100 etc.

Example

To find the answer to $5009 - 2747$ we want to count on from 2747 until we reach 5009. Using a number line can help.

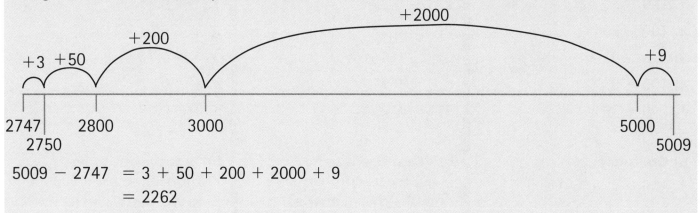

$$5009 - 2747 = 3 + 50 + 200 + 2000 + 9$$
$$= 2262$$

Method 2

Partitioning into 100s, 10s and 1s

This method can be used for addition and subtraction. We have already practised partitioning numbers and you will use this skill here. The number is partitioned to break the sum down into easier pieces.

Example

$643 + 26 =$
Instead of trying to add 26 straight away we will partition it and add it in pieces.

For addition:

$$643 + 26 = 643 + 20 + 6$$
$$= 663 + 6$$
$$= 669$$

For subtraction:

$$587 - 36 = 587 - 30 - 6$$
$$= 557 - 6$$
$$= 551$$

Mental calculations

Use the methods described on page 30 to answer these questions.

Bronze

a) Use Method 1 to solve these. You may find a number line will help you.

1. 69 − 42 =
2. 84 − 56 =
3. 92 − 37 =
4. 126 − 98 =
5. 163 − 75 =

b) Use Method 2 to solve these additions:

1. 36 + 23 =
2. 61 + 37 =
3. 45 + 44 =
4. 78 + 16 =
5. 52 + 39 =

c) Use Method 2 to solve these subtractions:

1. 78 − 24 =
2. 83 − 31 =
3. 92 − 62 =
4. 54 − 33 =
5. 42 − 25 =

Silver

a) Use Method 1 to solve these:

1. 704 − 358 =
2. 638 − 462 =
3. 8006 − 2993 =
4. 3205 − 1845 =
5. 5020 − 2786 =

b) Use Method 2 to solve these additions and subtractions:

1. 462 + 29 =
2. 639 +52 =
3. 476 + 37 =
4. 643 − 28 =
5. 532 − 19 =

c) Choose the method you think is best for these sums:

1. 453 − 28 =
2. 804 − 378 =
3. 6050 − 3766 =
4. 439 + 52 =
5. 628 + 65 =

Gold

a) Use Method 1 to solve these:

1. 6005 − 4989 =
2. 8034 − 3687 =
3. 6230 − 5821 =
4. 7015 − 3962 =
5. 3626 − 1945 =

b) Use Method 2 to solve these:

1. 462 + 229 =
2. 639 + 352 =
3. 476 + 537 =
4. 643 − 328 =
5. 532 − 219 =

c) Copy and complete these. Choose the most appropriate method.

1. 3000 − ☐ = 1437
2. 562 + ☐ = 673
3. 845 − ☐ = 327
4. 6008 − ☐ = 4255
5. 362 + ☐ = 891

Training Tips

 Counting up is a good method to use when the two numbers are close together.

 Take care to check the sum carefully – is it an addition or a subtraction?

Mental strategies

To solve these sums you are going to use the following two methods.

Method 1

Identify near doubles

For this method look for a number you can double then adjust.

Example

2.1 + 2.2 =

As 2.2 is very close to 2.1 we can double 2.1 and then adjust.

2.2 is 0.1 more than 2.1 so we add 0.1

So

$$2.1 + 2.2 = (2.1 \times 2) + 0.1$$
$$= 4.2 + 0.1$$
$$= 4.3$$

Method 2

Add or subtract the nearest multiple of 10 or 100 and adjust

For this method round the sum to the nearest 10 or 100, carry out the sum and then adjust.

Example

745 + 98 =

98 is 2 less than 100 so if we add 100 and adjust by subtracting 2 it would be easier.

$$745 + 98 = 745 + 100 - 2$$
$$= 845 - 2$$
$$= 843$$

$$4637 - 1998 = 4637 - 2000 + 2$$
$$= 2637 + 2$$
$$= 2639$$

Mental strategies

Use the methods described on page 32 to answer these questions.

Bronze

a) Use Method 1 to solve the following:

1. 2.3 + 2.4 =

2. 4.1 + 4.1 =

3. 2.1 + 2.3 =

4. 3.3 + 3.6 =

5. 4.4 + 4.5 =

b) Use Method 2 to solve these additions:

1. 54 + 19 =

2. 71 + 29 =

3. 24 + 47 =

4. 62 + 31 =

5. 36 + 48 =

c) Use Method 2 to solve these subtractions:

1. 96 − 39 =

2. 73 − 29 =

3. 58 − 18 =

4. 42 − 21 =

5. 65 − 47 =

Silver

a) Use Method 1 to solve the following:

1. 2.3 + 2.5 =

2. 6.1 + 6.3 =

3. 2.8 + 2.6 =

4. 3.6 + 3.7 =

5. 4.7 + 4.5 =

b) Use Method 2 to solve these additions:

1. 584 + 19 =

2. 761 + 29 =

3. 274 + 47 =

4. 692 + 101 =

5. 346 + 148 =

c) Use Method 2 to solve these subtractions:

1. 596 − 39 =

2. 713 − 29 =

3. 563 − 18 =

4. 462 − 21 =

5. 635 − 417 =

Gold

a) Use Method 1 to solve the following:

1. 8.3 + 8.5 =

2. 5.1 + 5.3 =

3. 6.8 + 6.6 =

4. 7.6 + 7.7 =

5. 9.7 + 9.5 =

b) Use Method 2 to solve these additions:

1. 5684 + 199 =

2. 7561 + 298 =

3. 2374 + 417 =

4. 6952 + 1001 =

5. 3346 + 1098 =

c) Use Method 2 to solve these subtractions:

1. 5926 − 309 =

2. 7413 − 229 =

3. 5363 − 189 =

4. 4762 − 2461 =

5. 6835 − 4312 =

Training Tips

 Doubling is the same as multiplying by 2.

Remember to adjust! **Look out for near doubles.**

Mental strategies

If you know 13 + 23 = 36, then you also know the following:

23 + 13 = 36   36 − 13 = 23   36 − 23 = 13

Practise finding these related facts on this page.

Bronze

For each given statement, complete the other related facts.

43 + 21 = 64

1. ☐ + 43 = ☐
2. 64 − ☐ = 21
3. 64 − ☐ = ☐

38 + 59 = 97

4. ☐ + ☐ = 97
5. 97 − ☐ = ☐
6. 97 − ☐ = ☐

72 − 43 = 29

7. 72 − ☐ = 43
8. 43 + ☐ = ☐
9. ☐ + ☐ = 72

94 − 56 = 38

10. 94 − ☐ = ☐
11. 56 + ☐ = ☐
12. ☐ + 56 = ☐

73 + 64 = 137

13. ☐ + ☐ = ☐
14. ☐ − ☐ = ☐
15. ☐ − ☐ = ☐

Silver

a) For each of these statements, write the three related facts.

1. 53 + 39 = 92
2. 163 + 389 = 552
3. 842 + 864 = 1706
4. 7374 − 2543 = 4831
5. 7309 − 3361 = 3948
6. 0.23 + 0.46 = 0.69
7. 7.8 − 2.4 = 5.4
8. 81.34 − 66.27 = 15.07
9. 68.82 + 123.65 = 192.47
10. 1396 + 4687 = 6083

b) Complete these statements and write the three related facts.

1. 3.5 + 3.6 =
2. 614 − 396 =
3. 627 + 68 =
4. 5002 + 2998 =
5. 12.21 + 11.36 =

Gold

a) For each of these statements, write the three related facts.

1. 1345 + 6544 = 7889
2. 9458 − 3599 = 5859
3. 13.65 + 67.47 = 81.12
4. 42.71 − 26.75 = 15.96
5. 8932 + 4677 =13 609

b) Complete these statements and write the three related facts.

1. 3465 + 2347 =
2. 12.34 + 32.13 =
3. 26.34 + 81.65 =
4. 72.43 − 35.31 =
5. 8945 − 3573 =

c) For each set of numbers, write four addition and subtraction statements.

1. 213, 412, 625
2. 735, 765, 30
3. 432, 938, 506
4. 37.25, 98.20, 135.45
5. 23.75, 13.04, 36.79

Training Tips

Check your answers by using the reverse operation.

For every subtraction or addition statement there are always three others.

Mental strategies

To **add several numbers** together it is useful to try the following:

- Start adding with the largest number.
- Look for pairs of numbers that make 10 or 100.
- Look for near doubles or facts you know.

Bronze

a) Add these numbers:

1. 6 + 5 + 4 + 2
2. 2 + 7 + 8 + 3
3. 20 + 30 + 80 + 10
4. 40 + 20 + 10 + 90
5. 20 + 60 + 50 + 50

Use any mental strategy to work out the answers to the following sums.

b) Add 11 to each of these:

1. 43
2. 52
3. 36
4. 124
5. 679

c) Subtract 9 from these:

1. 58
2. 39
3. 25
4. 427
5. 356

Silver

a) Answer these sums:

1. 5 + 6 + 7 + 8 + 5 =
2. 6 + 6 + 6 + 7 + 7 =
3. 50 + 30 + 50 + 20 + 40 =
4. 42 + 41 + 45 + 42 =
5. 56 + 21 + 44 + 32 =

Use any mental strategy to work out the answers to the following sums.

b) Add 42 to each of these:

1. 252
2. 168
3. 383
4. 575
5. 876

c) Subtract 59 from each of these:

1. 184
2. 320
3. 736
4. 489
5. 275

Gold

a) Add up each set of numbers:

1. 23, 24, 26, 23, 23
2. 12, 45, 82, 34, 11
3. 90, 30, 50, 40, 10
4. 400, 200, 400, 600, 800
5. 800, 700, 200, 600, 100

b) Copy and complete:

1. 11 + ☐ + 9 + 8 + 7 = 39
2. 80 + 60 + 20 + ☐ = 200
3. ☐ + 600 + 500 + 800 = 2600
4. 23 + 23 + 24 + ☐ = 83
5. 300 + 500 + ☐ + 400 = 1700

c) Using any mental strategy, work out:

1. ☐ + 198 = 647
2. 15.63 + ☐ = 18.72
3. 76.45 − ☐ = 45.32
4. ☐ − 482 = 216
5. 1265 + 3273 = ☐

Training Tips

Make sure you know what you have already added. Don't add the same number twice.

Start with the largest number and check by adding in a different order.

Written methods for addition

On this page you will practise using a written method for addition. Here are two methods you may use:

1. Partitioning

$$326 \longrightarrow 300 + 20 + 6$$
$$+254 \longrightarrow 200 + 50 + 4$$
$$\overline{500 + 70 + 10} \longrightarrow 580$$

2. Standard method

$$326 \longrightarrow 3 \ 2 \ 6$$
$$+254 \longrightarrow 2 \ 5 \ 4$$
$$\overline{5 \ 8 \ 0} \longrightarrow 580$$
$$_1$$

Bronze

a) Use your method to find the answer for each sum.

1. 43 + 52 =
2. 68 + 43 =
3. 35 + 28 =
4. 94 + 25 =
5. 843 + 52 =
6. 364 + 27 =
7. 632 + 49 =
8. 236 + 541 =
9. 672 + 327 =
10. 555 + 362 =

b) Work out these word problems:

1. Carly buys 24 apples and Sonja buys 28. How many apples do they buy altogether?

2. Mark plays 43 games of football. Geoff plays 11 more. How many games has Geoff played?

Silver

a) Use your method to find the answer for each sum.

1. 443 + 542 =
2. 628 + 283 =
3. 365 + 228 =
4. 954 + 249 =
5. 8413 + 452 =
6. 3684 + 227 =
7. 6632 + 495 =
8. 6236 + 3541 =
9. 1672 + 7327 =
10. 5453 + 5362 =

b) Work out these word problems:

1. Ben and Armhet collect football stickers. Ben has 324 stickers and Armhet has 267. What is the sum of their collection?

2. Lisa flew 6345 miles and then drove 327 miles. How long was her journey?

Gold

a) Use your method to find the answer for each sum.

1. 4643 + 5342 =
2. 6248 + 2983 =
3. 3645 + 2628 =
4. 9154 + 2469 =
5. 7413 + 5452 =
6. 6286 + 9541 =
7. 3672 + 6327 =
8. 5453 + 9362 =
9. 36854 + 7227 =
10. 63832 + 4965 =

b) Work out these word problems:

1. The shopkeeper sold 457 Mars bars, 623 Bounty bars and 563 KitKats. How many chocolate bars did he sell in total?

2. There were 127 red tables and 643 grey tables in the hall. How many tables were there altogether?

Training Tips

Practise your method regularly so you get quicker.

Watch out when you are adding across boundaries that you don't make a mistake.

Adding decimals

Adding **decimals** is exactly the same as adding other numbers.
You can still use the method you would normally use.

1. Partitioning

$$5.32 \longrightarrow 5 + 0.3 + 0.02$$
$$+4.83 \longrightarrow \underline{4 + 0.8 + 0.03}$$
$$9 + 1.1 + 0.05 \longrightarrow 10.15$$

2. Standard method

$$5.32 \longrightarrow 5 \ . \ 3 \ 2$$
$$+4.83 \longrightarrow \underline{4 \ . \ 8 \ 3}$$
$$10 \ . \ 1 \ 5 \longrightarrow 10.15$$
$$ 1$$

Bronze

Solve these:

1. 2.4 + 3.3 =
2. 1.3 + 2.4 =
3. 3.2 + 2.5 =
4. 1.7 + 7.2 =
5. 1.5 + 5.2 =
6. 7.4 + 2.3 =
7. 5.1 + 3.7 =
8. 6.4 + 2.5 =
9. 4.4 + 5.3 =
10. 3.4 + 1.9 =
11. £7.20 + £1.50 =
12. £2.30 + £4.60 =
13. £6.60 + £3.20 =
14. £5.10 + £2.50 =
15. £3.80 + £1.30 =

Silver

Solve these:

1. 7.64 + 2.25 =
2. 2.91 + 4.04 =
3. 1.17 + 6.17 =
4. 3.22 + 5.27 =
5. 0.62 + 1.12 =
6. 2.28 + 4.63 =
7. 1.64 + 6.28 =
8. 5.14 + 2.56 =
9. 3.68 + 2.17 =
10. 6.24 + 2.19 =
11. £5.44 + £2.94 =
12. £6.62 + £3.60 =
13. £2.58 + £4.81 =
14. £2.61 + £5.94 =
15. £7.65 + £2.44 =

Gold

Solve these:

1. 7.44 + 2.71 =
2. 3.84 + 4.33 =
3. 3.52 + 4.63 =
4. 5.61 + 1.54 =
5. 4.83 + 1.95 =
6. 2.66 + 3.75 =
7. 6.97 + 1.45 =
8. 2.74 + 3.47 =
9. 1.86 + 6.35 =
10. 4.82 + 1.49 =
11. £2.75 + £3.47 =
12. £5.93 + £3.28 =
13. £1.83 + £4.27 =
14. £4.66 + £3.55 =
15. £7.76 + £2.37 =

Training Tips

Think of decimals as amounts of money.

Remember the £ sign when answering money questions.

Written methods for subtraction

Here are two methods you may use:

1. Partitioning

$$892 \longrightarrow 800 + 90 + 2$$
$$-365 \longrightarrow \underline{300 + 60 + 5}$$
$$500 + 20 + 7$$

2. Standard method

$$892 \longrightarrow 8\ ^8\!\!\not{9}\ ^1 2$$
$$-365 \longrightarrow \underline{3\ \ 6\ \ 5}$$
$$5\ \ 2\ \ 7$$

Bronze

a) Use your method to find the answer for each sum.

1. 64 − 33 =
2. 86 − 43 =
3. 65 − 24 =
4. 198 − 25 =
5. 863 − 32 =

b) Now try these. Watch out for the traps!

1. 64 − 27 =
2. 72 − 45 =
3. 46 − 23 =
4. 372 − 91 =
5. 675 − 283 =

c) Work out these word problems:

1. Claire has 42 sweets. She eats 11. How many does she have left?

2. There are 89 children in the pool. 25 children get out. What is the total number of children left in the pool?

Silver

a) Use your method to find the answer for each sum.

1. 464 − 233 =
2. 986 − 543 =
3. 365 − 124 =
4. 898 − 225 =
5. 863 − 732 =

b) Now try these. Watch out for the traps!

1. 564 − 227 =
2. 972 − 145 =
3. 746 − 323 =
4. 372 − 281 =
5. 984 − 392 =

c) Work out this word problem:

There were 349 people on the school trip from two different schools. There were 276 people from one school. How many people were from the other school?

Gold

a) Use your method to find the answer for each sum.

1. 6564 − 2331 =
2. 8846 − 4325 =
3. 6255 − 2143 =
4. 7398 − 2256 =
5. 8663 − 3251 =

b) Now try these. Watch out for the traps!

1. 6473 − 4227 =
2. 7279 − 4185 =
3. 4654 − 2732 =
4. 3724 − 1915 =
5. 6754 − 2869 =

c) Work out this word problem:

Farmer Ringer had a piece of string 3655 mm long. He cut off a piece 1589 mm long. How much does he have left?

 **Training Tips**

 It doesn't matter what method you use, as long as it works for you!

 Watch you don't fall into the subtraction trap!

Subtracting decimals

Subtracting decimals is exactly the same as subtracting other numbers.
You can still use the method you would normally use.

1. Partitioning

$$6.45 \longrightarrow 6 + 0.4 + 0.05$$
$$-4.52 \longrightarrow 4 + 0.5 + 0.02$$
$$\overline{1 + 0.9 + 0.03} \longrightarrow 1.93$$

2. Standard method

$$6.45 \longrightarrow {}^5\cancel{6} \,.\, {}^14 \; 5$$
$$-4.52 \longrightarrow \underline{4 \,.\, 5 \; 2}$$
$$1 \,.\, 9 \; 3 \longrightarrow 1.93$$

Bronze	Silver	Gold
Solve these:	**Solve these:**	**Solve these:**
1. 9.9 − 7.2 =	**1.** 5.64 − 2.21 =	**1.** 7.63 − 4.07 =
2. 1.8 − 1.3 =	**2.** 6.47 − 4.15 =	**2.** 2.50 − 1.04 =
3. 6.8 − 4.3 =	**3.** 4.39 − 1.17 =	**3.** 7.21 − 6.02 =
4. 5.7 − 2.4 =	**4.** 6.94 − 5.22 =	**4.** 8.76 − 7.59 =
5. 4.7 − 2.4 =	**5.** 9.74 − 6.43 =	**5.** 7.97 − 4.89 =
6. 2.6 − 1.3 =	**6.** 2.94 − 1.77 =	**6.** 2.37 − 1.79 =
7. 7.4 − 4.3 =	**7.** 6.83 − 3.57 =	**7.** 6.54 − 2.68 =
8. 3.6 − 1.5 =	**8.** 3.36 − 1.55 =	**8.** 5.20 − 1.78 =
9. 4.6 − 2.6 =	**9.** 3.71 − 2.38 =	**9.** 5.41 − 2.54 =
10. 2.9 − 1.6 =	**10.** 8.38 − 2.47 =	**10.** 4.15 − 1.89 =
11. £6.58 − £3.25 =	**11.** £7.64 − £6.39 =	**11.** £6.06 − £4.77 =
12. £8.47 − £5.14 =	**12.** £2.44 − £1.63 =	**12.** £7.31 − £3.57 =
13. £5.48 − £4.13 =	**13.** £7.57 − £4.38 =	**13.** £6.23 − £1.64 =
14. £7.54 − £2.24 =	**14.** £8.50 − £6.42 =	**14.** £5.10 − £2.65 =
15. £5.58 − £1.37 =	**15.** £3.21 − £2.19 =	**15.** £8.00 − £4.87 =

 **Training Tips**

 Watch out for subtraction traps!

 Think of decimals as amounts of money to help you.

Understanding multiplication and division

If you know $3 \times 6 = 18$, then you also know the following:

$6 \times 3 = 18$	$18 \div 6 = 3$	$18 \div 3 = 6$

You are going to practise finding these related facts on this page.

Bronze

For each given statement, complete three other related facts.

$5 \times 7 = 35$

1. $\square \times 5 = \square$
2. $35 \div \square = 7$
3. $35 \div \square = \square$

$8 \times 9 = 72$

4. $\square \times \square = 72$
5. $72 \div \square = \square$
6. $72 \div \square = \square$

$24 \div 6 = 4$

7. $24 \div \square = 6$
8. $6 \times \square = \square$
9. $\square \times \square = 24$

$27 \div 3 = 9$

10. $27 \div \square = \square$
11. $3 \times \square = \square$
12. $\square \times 3 = \square$

$2 \times 13 = 26$

13. $\square \times \square = \square$
14. $\square \div \square = \square$
15. $\square \div \square = \square$

Silver

a) For each of these statements, write the three related facts.

1. $6 \times 9 = 54$
2. $56 \div 7 = 8$
3. $12 \times 2 = 24$
4. $25 \times 4 = 100$
5. $42 \div 6 = 7$

b) Complete these statements and write the three related facts.

1. $5 \times 6 =$
2. $7 \times 9 =$
3. $24 \div 2 =$
4. $4 \times 7 =$
5. $21 \div 3 =$

c) Copy and complete:

1. $2 \times \square = 36$
2. $\square \times 9 = 27$
3. $36 \div \square = 6$
4. $\square \div 10 = 10$
5. $13 \times \square = 39$

Gold

a) Complete these statements and write the three related facts.

1. $3 \times 7 =$
2. $9 \times 8 =$
3. $5 \times 9 =$
4. $12 \times 5 =$
5. $11 \times 8 =$

b) Write four statements for each set of numbers.

1. 20, 8, 160
2. 90, 6, 15
3. 28, 4, 112
4. 11, 12, 132
5. 60, 40, 2400

c) Copy and complete:

1. $15 \times \square = 135$
2. $\square \times 9 = 63$
3. $104 \div \square = 13$
4. $\square \div 6 = 20$
5. $12 \times \square = 96$

Training Tips

Always remember that multiplication is the opposite of division.

Check your answers by using the reverse operation.

Brackets

Brackets are very useful when you have a sum with more than one step.
We put brackets around the part of the sum that needs to be done first.

Example
$20 - (3 \times 6) = 20 - 18 = 2$
We solved the brackets first, then the rest of the sum.

Bronze

a) Solve:

1. $10 + (2 \times 2) =$

2. $10 - (3 \times 2) =$

3. $10 - (4 \times 2) =$

4. $10 + (5 \times 2) =$

5. $10 - (1 \times 7) =$

b) Solve:

1. $(2 \times 10) + 8 =$

2. $(6 \times 5) - 20 =$

3. $(4 \times 2) + 6 =$

4. $(5 \times 20) + 50 =$

5. $(10 \times 5) - 20 =$

c) True or false?

1. $3 + (5 \times 3) = 18$

2. $4 + (9 \times 2) = 20$

3. $(2 \times 3) + 8 = 14$

4. $20 + (4 \times 3) = 31$

5. $(4 + 1) \times 6 = 30$

Silver

a) Work out:

1. $10 \times (21 - 4)$

2. $(3 \times 6) + 17 =$

3. $8 \times (2 + 3) =$

4. $(8 \times 7) - 12 =$

5. $9 \times (8 - 6) =$

b) Solve:

1. $(24 \div 2) + 25 =$

2. $(66 \div 11) \times 5 =$

3. $100 - (54 \div 9) =$

4. $25 + (45 \div 9) =$

5. $(60 \div 4) - 9 =$

c) True or false?

1. $(2 \times 3) + (3 \times 5) = 20$

2. $(8 \times 7) - (4 \times 2) = 48$

3. $(36 \div 9) + (2 \times 5) = 15$

4. $(5 \times 8) + (11 \times 6) = 106$

5. $(10 \times 11) - (30 \div 5) = 104$

Gold

a) Solve:

1. $2 \times (5 + 7 + 8)$

2. $2 \times (6 + 7 + 8)$

3. $10 \times (9 + 8 + 7 + 6)$

4. $5 \times (9 - 7 + 4)$

5. $5 \times (11 + 6 - 9)$

b) Work out:

1. $(42 \div 7) + 11 =$

2. $26 + (5 \times 11) =$

3. $20 + (144 \div 12) =$

4. $(8 \times 7) + 35 =$

5. $75 \div (3 \times 5) =$

c) Solve:

1. $(3 \times 6) + (4 \times 2) =$

2. $(5 \times 8) + (3 \times 9) =$

3. $(9 \times 9) - (3 \times 6) =$

4. $(11 \times 10) - (5 \times 4) =$

5. $(7 \times 7) - (6 \times 6) =$

Training Tips

 Always work out the brackets first.

 Try to use brackets in your work when you use more than one operation.

Remainders

When we **divide** one number by another it can either divide exactly or leave **remainders**.
For example: $25 \div 5 = 5$. There are no remainders.

> $25 \div 4 = 6$ remainder 1.

That means 4 goes into 25 six times with 1 left over.
We often give the answer 6 r 1 where r stands for remainder.

Bronze

a) Match the answer for each sum to its remainder equivalent:

1. $45 \div 10 = 4$ r 5 $4\frac{2}{5}$
2. $9 \div 2 = 4$ r 1   5.5
3. $22 \div 5 = 4$ r 2   4.6
4. $11 \div 2 = 5$ r 1 $4\frac{1}{2}$
5. $23 \div 5 = 4$ r 3   4.5

b) Give the remainder as a fraction:

1. $13 \div 2 =$
2. $27 \div 5 =$
3. $33 \div 2 =$
4. $17 \div 10 =$
5. $39 \div 5 =$

c) Give the remainder as a decimal:

1. £46 $\div$ 5 =
2. £25 $\div$ 2 =
3. £86 $\div$ 10 =
4. £53 $\div$ 10 =
5. £38 $\div$ 5 =

Silver

a) Give the remainder as a fraction:

1. $18 \div 4 =$
2. $78 \div 5 =$
3. $51 \div 8 =$
4. $46 \div 7 =$
5. $95 \div 10 =$

b) Give the remainder as a decimal:

1. £164 $\div$ 5 =
2. £490 $\div$ 10 =
3. £6.30 $\div$ 2 =
4. £7.70 $\div$ 4 =
5. £3.70 $\div$ 5 =

c) Give the remainder as a fraction and as a decimal:

1. $82 \div 4 =$
2. $124 \div 10 =$
3. $107 \div 5 =$
4. $126 \div 4 =$
5. $219 \div 2 =$

Gold

a) Give the remainder as a fraction:

1. $184 \div 6 =$
2. $174 \div 9 =$
3. $163 \div 8 =$
4. $135 \div 11 =$
5. $120 \div 7 =$

b) Give the remainder as a decimal:

1. £12.30 $\div$ 5 =
2. £45.60 $\div$ 4 =
3. £68.30 $\div$ 2 =
4. £17.50 $\div$ 4 =
5. £342.70 $\div$ 5 =

c) Give the remainder as a fraction and as a decimal:

1. $95 \div 4 =$
2. $1563 \div 10 =$
3. $4576 \div 5 =$
4. $920 \div 4 =$
5. $7849 \div 10 =$

Training Tips

Multiplication and division are opposites. Use multiplication to check your answers.

Look out for these division words: divide, remainder, quotient, share, divisible by.

Rounding up or down

When using division in word problems, it is important to make sensible decisions about whether to round the answer up or down.

Example
It costs £5 per person to get into the zoo. Jen has £32. How many people can Jen take into the zoo?
32 ÷ 5 = 6 r 2   We **round down** to 6 people.

A CD rack holds 20 CDs. How many CD racks do I need to hold 83 CDs?
83 ÷ 20 = 4 r 3   I need 5 CD racks. We **round up** because 4 CD racks would leave 3 CDs.

Bronze

a) **Complete:**

1. 63 ÷ 5 =   (round up)

2. 41 ÷ 2 =   (round down)

3. 32 ÷ 3 =   (round up)

4. 54 ÷ 5 =   (round down)

5. 105 ÷ 10 = (round up)

b) **Complete:**

1. A car carries 5 people. How many cars do we need to carry 24 people?

2. A CD rack holds 40 CDs. How many CD racks do we need to hold 74 CDs?

3. It costs £10 to get into the theme park. Sam has £95. How many people can Sam take to the theme park?

4. Bags of sweets cost £4 each. Sarah has £15. How many bags of sweets can Sarah buy?

Silver

a) **Complete:**

1. 84 ÷ 9 =   (round up)

2. 64 ÷ 6 =   (round down)

3. 37 ÷ 4 =   (round up)

4. 62 ÷ 5 =   (round down)

5. 28 ÷ 3 =   (round up)

b) **Complete:**

1. A van carries 3 people. How many vans do we need to carry 25 people?

2. A CD rack holds 9 CDs. How many CD racks do we need to hold 74 CDs?

3. It costs £7 to get into the theme park. Sam has £67. How many people can Sam take to the theme park?

4. Bags of sweets cost £5 each. Sarah has £87. How many bags of sweets can Sarah buy?

Gold

a) **Complete:**

1. 76 ÷ 12 =   (round up)

2. 40 ÷ 15 =   (round down)

3. 108 ÷ 11 = (round up)

4. 75 ÷ 7 =   (round down)

5. 75 ÷ 8 =   (round up)

b) **Complete:**

1. A minibus carries 11 people. How many minibuses do we need to carry 60 people?

2. A CD rack holds 12 CDs. How many CD racks do we need to hold 75 CDs?

3. It costs £9 to get into the theme park. Sam has £85. How many people can Sam take to the theme park?

4. Bags of sweets cost £7 each. Sarah has £61. How many bags of sweets can Sarah buy?

Training Tips

Drawing pictures could help you to decide whether to round up or down.

Take care when writing division sums (usually larger number ÷ smaller number).

Multiplication and division facts

Learning your **times tables** is an important skill.
Use your times table knowledge to solve these questions.

Bronze

a) Write answers only:

1. 3 × 5 =

2. 4 × 6 =

3. 2 × 8 =

4. 9 × 5 =

5. 4 × 3 =

b) Write answers only:

1. 30 ÷ 10

2. 25 ÷ 5

3. 18 ÷ 2

4. 18 ÷ 3

5. 24 ÷ 4

c) Match each sum to its answer:

1. 35 ÷ 5 =   18

2. 10 × 6 =   8

3. 6 × 3 =   40

4. 24 ÷ 3 =   7

5. 5 × 8 =   60

Silver

a) Write answers only:

1. 4 × 7 =

2. 6 × 4 =

3. 8 × 6 =

4. 9 × 4 =

5. 3 × 8 =

b) Write answers only:

1. 42 ÷ 6 =

2. 72 ÷ 9 =

3. 48 ÷ 8 =

4. 63 ÷ 7 =

5. 63 ÷ 9 =

c) Copy and complete:

1. 7 × ☐ = 63

2. ☐ ÷ 4 = 8

3. ☐ × 8 = 56

4. ☐ ÷ 6 = 5

5. ☐ ÷ 7 = 6

Gold

a) Write answers only:

1. 9 × 0.8 =

2. 6 × 0.3 =

3. 0.7 × 6 =

4. 0.3 × 9 =

5. 4 × 0.6 =

b) Write answers only:

1. 4.9 ÷ 7 =

2. 2.4 ÷ 8 =

3. 4.2 ÷ 6 =

4. 6.3 ÷ 9 =

5. 2.8 ÷ 4 =

c) Copy and complete:

1. 0.7 × ☐ = 4.2

2. ☐ ÷ 4 = 0.5

3. ☐ × 8 = 4.8

4. ☐ ÷ 6 = 0.6

5. ☐ ÷ 7 = 0.9

Training Tips

Remember 3 x 4 and 4 x 3 are the same.

Multiplication and division are opposites. Use times table facts to solve division questions.

Doubling and halving

To **double** a number, multiply it by 2.

$36 \times 2 = 72$

If you need to double larger numbers, partition them: 135×2

$$135 = 100 + 30 + 5$$
$$\text{Double } 135 = (100 \times 2) + (30 \times 2) + (5 \times 2)$$
$$= 200 + 60 + 10$$
$$= 270$$

To **halve** a number, divide it by 2.

$72 \div 2 = 36$

If you need to halve a larger number, partitioning can help: $270 \div 2$

$$270 = 200 + 70$$
$$\text{Half } 270 = (200 \div 2) + (70 \div 2)$$
$$= 100 + 35$$
$$= 135$$

Bronze

a) **Double the following:**

1. 13
2. 24
3. 16
4. 120
5. 1000

b) **Halve the following:**

1. 48
2. 24
3. 50
4. 260
5. 6000

c) **Complete the following:**

1. $15 \times 2 =$
2. $64 \div 2 =$
3. $27 \times 2 =$
4. $76 \div 2 =$
5. $38 \times 2 =$

Silver

a) **Double the following:**

1. 43
2. 52
3. 250
4. 370
5. 1600

b) **Halve the following:**

1. 76
2. 112
3. 164
4. 570
5. 1240

c) **Complete the following:**

1. $140 \times 2 =$
2. $2800 \div 2 =$
3. $270 \div 2 =$
4. $1900 \times 2 =$
5. $470 \times 2 =$

Gold

a) **Double the following:**

1. 739
2. 1580
3. 3.6
4. 7.8
5. 19 700

b) **Halve the following:**

1. 15 600
2. 5.6
3. 12 800
4. 23 400
5. 9.8

c) **Complete the following:**

1. $6800 \times 2 =$
2. $1.42 \div 2 =$
3. $35 400 \times 2 =$
4. $8.65 \times 2 =$
5. $12 500 \div 2 =$

 **Training Tips**

Double $\times 2$
Halve $\div 2$

Partition the numbers to help you.

Using doubling and halving

You can use **doubling and halving** to solve calculations.

If you know $2 \times 8 = 16$ then, by doubling, $2 \times 16 = 32$

If you know $4 \times 12 = 48$ then, by halving, $2 \times 12 = 24$ and $4 \times 6 = 24$

Bronze

a) **Work out the 16 times table by doubling these facts from the 8 times table:**

1. $3 \times 8 = 24$ $3 \times 16 = \square$

2. $4 \times 8 = 32$ $4 \times 16 = \square$

3. $5 \times 8 = 40$ $5 \times 16 = \square$

4. $6 \times 8 = 48$ $6 \times 16 = \square$

5. $10 \times 8 = 80$ $10 \times 16 = \square$

b) **Work out the following fractions by halving:**

1. $\frac{1}{2}$ of $12 = 6$
$\frac{1}{4}$ of $12 = \square$

2. $\frac{1}{2}$ of $28 = 14$
$\frac{1}{4}$ of $28 = \square$

3. $\frac{1}{2}$ of $44 = 22$
$\frac{1}{4}$ of $44 = \square$

4. $\frac{1}{2}$ of $100 = 50$
$\frac{1}{4}$ of $100 = \square$

5. $\frac{1}{2}$ of $300 = 150$
$\frac{1}{4}$ of $300 = \square$

Silver

a) **Work out the 18 times table by doubling these facts from the 9 times table:**

1. $3 \times 9 = 27$ $3 \times 18 = \square$

2. $8 \times 9 = 72$ $8 \times 18 = \square$

3. $7 \times 9 = 63$ $7 \times 18 = \square$

4. $6 \times 9 = 54$ $6 \times 18 = \square$

5. $9 \times 9 = 81$ $9 \times 18 = \square$

b) **Work out the following by doubling or halving:**

1. $17 \times 4 =$ **2.** $84 \div 4 =$

3. $36 \times 5 =$ **4.** $400 \div 5 =$

c) **Find a third of the numbers given and then find a sixth by halving:**

1. $\frac{1}{3}$ of $18 =$ $\frac{1}{6}$ of $18 =$

2. $\frac{1}{3}$ of $66 =$ $\frac{1}{6}$ of $66 =$

3. $\frac{1}{3}$ of $90 =$ $\frac{1}{6}$ of $90 =$

4. $\frac{1}{3}$ of $120 =$ $\frac{1}{6}$ of $120 =$

5. $\frac{1}{3}$ of $600 =$ $\frac{1}{6}$ of $600 =$

Gold

a) **Work out the 36 times table by doubling the 18 times table:**

1. $2 \times 18 =$ $2 \times 36 =$

2. $3 \times 18 =$ $3 \times 36 =$

3. $5 \times 18 =$ $5 \times 36 =$

4. $6 \times 18 =$ $6 \times 36 =$

5. $7 \times 18 =$ $7 \times 36 =$

b) **Work out the following by doubling or halving:**

1. $17 \times 8 =$ **2.** $184 \div 4 =$

3. $360 \times 5 =$ **4.** $4000 \div 25 =$

c) **Using the facts given find a sixth and a twelfth:**

1. $\frac{1}{3}$ of $96 = 32$
$\frac{1}{6}$ of $96 = \square$
$\frac{1}{12}$ of $96 = \square$

2. $\frac{1}{3}$ of $150 = 50$
$\frac{1}{6}$ of $150 = \square$
$\frac{1}{12}$ of $150 = \square$

3. $\frac{1}{3}$ of $6000 = 2000$
$\frac{1}{6}$ of $6000 = \square$
$\frac{1}{12}$ of $6000 = \square$

Training Tips

$\times 4 =$ double, then double again.
$\div 4 =$ halve, then halve again.

You will find you know more times tables than you think by doubling and halving.

Mental strategies

1. Using factors

Example

Look at the sum and find factors

$$16 \times 5 = (2 \times 8) \times 5$$

Rearrange the sum to make it easier

$$= 2 \times (8 \times 5)$$
$$= 2 \times 40$$
$$= 80$$

2. Multiplying by 19 or 21

To multiply by 19 or 21 we multiply by 20 and then adjust.

Example

$$12 \times 19 = (12 \times 20) - (12 \times 1)$$
$$= 240 - 12$$
$$= 228$$

Bronze

a) Use factors to solve:

1. $7 \times 8 = 7 \times (\square \times 2)$
$= (7 \times \square) \times 2 = \square$

2. $12 \times 6 = 12 \times (\square \times 2)$
$= (12 \times \square) \times 2 = \square$

3. $14 \times 4 = 14 \times (\square \times 2)$
$= (14 \times \square) \times 2 = \square$

4. $12 \times 8 = \square$

5. $14 \times 6 = \square$

b) Use factors to solve:

1. $64 \div 8 = 64 \div (2 \times \square)$
$= (64 \div 2) \div \square = \square$

2. $48 \div 6 = 48 \div (2 \times \square)$
$= (48 \div 2) \div \square = \square$

3. $60 \div 4 = 60 \div (2 \times \square)$
$= (60 \div 2) \div \square = \square$

4. $72 \div 8 = \square$

5. $54 \div 6 = \square$

Silver

a) Use factors to solve:

1. $15 \times 8 =$

2. $17 \times 6 =$

3. $16 \times 12 =$

4. $18 \times 8 =$

5. $19 \times 6 =$

b) Use factors to solve:

1. $104 \div 8 =$

2. $84 \div 6 =$

3. $132 \div 12 =$

4. $112 \div 8 =$

5. $108 \div 6 =$

c) Work out:

1. $16 \times 19 =$

2. $12 \times 19 =$

3. $18 \times 21 =$

4. $14 \times 21 =$

5. $23 \times 21 =$

Gold

a) Use factors to solve:

1. $13 \times 12 =$

2. $16 \times 21 =$

3. $14 \times 18 =$

4. $17 \times 12 =$

5. $19 \times 21 =$

b) Use factors to solve:

1. $168 \div 12 =$

2. $273 \div 21 =$

3. $288 \div 18 =$

4. $228 \div 12 =$

5. $315 \div 21 =$

c) Work out:

1. $12 \times 39 =$

2. $15 \times 29 =$

3. $16 \times 41 =$

4. $18 \times 51 =$

5. $13 \times 71 =$

Training Tips

Factors are pairs of numbers that can be multiplied together to reach your target.

÷ 2 is the same as halving.

Mental Strategies

1. Partitioning
Partitioning can be used for multiplication too!
Example
12 x 7 = (10 x 7) + (2 x 7)
= 70 + 14 = 84

2. Adding
You can create a new times table by adding together two tables you already know!
Example
2 × 12 = 2 × 10 + 2 × 2 = 24

Bronze

a) Copy and complete:

1. 14 × 3 = (10×3) + (4×3) =
2. 16 × 5 = (10×5) + (6×5) =
3. 23 × 4 = (20×4) + (3×4) =
4. 18 × 3 = (10×3) + (8×3) =
5. 34 × 4 = (30×4) + (4×4) =
6. 41 × 5 = (40×5) + (1×5) =
7. 27 × 4 = (20×4) + (7×4) =
8. 53 × 3 = (50×3) + (3×3) =

b) Complete this table to create the 16 times table:

× 10	× 6	× 16
10	6	16
20	12	32
30	☐	☐
☐	24	☐
50	☐	80
☐	36	☐
☐	☐	112
☐	48	☐
90	☐	☐
☐	60	☐

Silver

a) Work out:

1. 18 × 6 = (10×6) + (8×6) =
2. 19 × 8 = (10×3) + (9×8) =
3. 27 × 7 =
4. 18 × 9 =
5. 49 × 7 =
6. 56 × 6 =
7. 67 × 9 =
8. 53 × 8 =

b) Complete this table to create the 18 times table:

× 8	× 10	× 18
8	10	18
16	20	36
☐	☐	☐
☐	☐	☐
40	☐	☐
☐	☐	☐
☐	☐	☐
64	☐	☐
☐	☐	☐
80	☐	☐

Gold

a) Work out:

1. 88 × 6 =
2. 69 × 8 =
3. 97 × 7 =
4. 78 × 9 =
5. 49 × 7 =
6. 3.2 × 6 =
7. 6.7 × 9 =
8. 5.3 × 8 =
9. 8.2 × 6 =
10. 7.4 × 7 =

b) Complete this table to create the 23 times table:

× 13	× 10	× 23
13	10	23
26	20	46

Training Tips

 Try making new times tables by adding.

 Remember × 10 – each digit moves one place to the left.

Mental strategies

Place value

You can solve multiplication and division questions by using your knowledge of place value and your times tables.

If you know	$3 \times 6 = 18$
Then you also know	$3 \times 60 = 180$
And...	$3 \times 600 = 1800$

Bronze

a) **Copy and complete:**

1. $4 \times 8 = 32$ $4 \times 80 =$
2. $3 \times 9 = 27$ $3 \times 90 =$
3. $6 \times 7 = 42$ $6 \times 70 =$
4. $7 \times 5 = 35$ $7 \times 50 =$
5. $6 \times 4 = 24$ $6 \times 40 =$

b) **Match the sums with the answers:**

1. $16 \times 10 =$ 360
2. $8 \times 50 =$ 120
3. $4 \times 30 =$ 400
4. $3 \times 70 =$ 160
5. $6 \times 60 =$ 210

c) **Complete:**

1. $6 \times 40 =$
2. $5 \times 30 =$
3. $3 \times 70 =$
4. $4 \times 80 =$
5. $4 \times 60 =$

Silver

a) **Copy and complete:**

1. $6 \times 8 =$ $6 \times 80 =$
   $6 \times 800 =$
2. $7 \times 9 =$ $7 \times 90 =$
   $7 \times 900 =$
3. $5 \times 7 =$ $5 \times 70 =$
   $5 \times 700 =$
4. $8 \times 5 =$ $8 \times 50 =$
   $8 \times 500 =$
5. $9 \times 4 =$ $9 \times 40 =$
   $9 \times 400 =$

b) **Work out:**

1. $7 \times 80 =$
2. $4 \times 70 =$
3. $9 \times 600 =$
4. $8 \times 900 =$
5. $7 \times 700 =$

c) **Work out:**

1. $180 \div 20 =$
2. $5500 \div 50 =$
3. $2700 \div 300 =$
4. $4800 \div 600 =$
5. $49\,000 \div 700 =$

Gold

a) **Work out:**

1. $9 \times 30 =$
2. $8 \times 70 =$
3. $11 \times 600 =$
4. $12 \times 400 =$
5. $7 \times 8000 =$

b) **Work out:**

1. $5600 \div 70 =$
2. $1800 \div 60 =$
3. $400 \div 800 =$
4. $810 \div 900 =$
5. $7500 \div 5000 =$

c) **Solve:**

1. $\square \times 90 = 81\,000$
2. $\square \div 300 = 140$
3. $1.5 \times \square = 3$
4. $7200 \div \square = 90$
5. $\square \times 50 = 75$

Training Tips

When you multiply by 10 each digit moves one place to the left.

When you divide by 10 each digit moves one place to the right.

The chunking method

One way of dividing is to think of it as **repeated subtraction**.

For example, 24 ÷ 4

If you subtract 4 from 24 **six times** you end up with 0. We know that 4 divides into 24 exactly with no remainder.

Now look at the example opposite using bigger numbers.

329 ÷ 6 =

Think what large 'chunk' of 6s we can take away.

```
 329
 300  – (50 x 6)
  29
  24  – (4 x 6)
   5
```

You cannot take away any more 6s as the number is less than 6.

So 6 goes into 329 fifty-four times (add the numbers in blue) with remainder 5.

Bronze

a) **Copy and complete:**

1. 33 ÷ 3 = 33 − (**10** × 3)
            3 − (**1** × 3)
            0

Answer:

2. 60 ÷ 5 = 60 − (× 5)
            10 − (× 5)
            0

Answer:

3. 65 ÷ 4 =

4. 75 ÷ 3 =

5. 63 ÷ 2 =

b) **Now practise the method with these sums:**

1. 85 ÷ 4 =   **2.** 62 ÷ 4 =

3. 46 ÷ 2 =   **4.** 34 ÷ 9 =

5. 49 ÷ 2 =

Silver

Using the chunking method, solve these:

1. 535 ÷ 6 =

2. 272 ÷ 5 =

3. 173 ÷ 4 =

4. 353 ÷ 3 =

5. 787 ÷ 8 =

6. 943 ÷ 5 =

7. 512 ÷ 9 =

8. 709 ÷ 7 =

9. 114 ÷ 8 =

10. 777 ÷ 6 =

11. 417 ÷ 4 =

12. 402 ÷ 8 =

13. 521 ÷ 7 =

14. 864 ÷ 9 =

15. 589 ÷ 6 =

Gold

a) **Using the chunking method, solve these:**

1. 6547 ÷ 6 =

2. 2795 ÷ 7 =

3. 3473 ÷ 4 =

4. 3578 ÷ 5 =

5. 8544 ÷ 3 =

6. 8053 ÷ 7 =

7. 9753 ÷ 8 =

8. 6854 ÷ 9 =

9. 4562 ÷ 6 =

10. 9452 ÷ 7 =

b) **Now try these:**

1. 233 ÷ 13 =

2. 389 ÷ 26 =

3. 234 ÷ 18 =

4. 748 ÷ 24 =

5. 638 ÷ 58 =

Training Tips

 Circle the numbers so that adding the 'chunks' is easy.

 Try to think of the biggest 'chunk' you can take away.

Grid method for multiplication

On this page you will practise using an informal written method for multiplication. It is called the grid method.

326 × 4 =

326	300	20	6		
×4	1200	80	24	=	1304

Method

1. Partition the numbers in the sum and draw a grid.
2. Carry out the multiplications.
3. Add up the answers (the numbers in grey boxes).

Bronze

a) Copy and complete:

1. 23 × 4 =

	20	3	
×4			=

2. 42 × 3 =

	40	2	
×3			=

3. 16 × 5 =

	10	6	
×5			=

4. 34 × 6 =

	30	4	
×6			=

5. 55 × 4 =

	50	5	
×4			=

b) Use the grid method to work these out (no grids to help this time):

1. 71 × 4 =

2. 63 × 3 =

3. 43 × 8 =

4. 36 × 7 =

5. 83 × 3 =

Silver

a) Copy and complete:

1. 263 × 5 =

	200	60	3	
×5				=

2. 432 × 6 =

	400	30	2	
×6				=

3. 166 × 7 =

	100	60	6	
×7				=

b) Use the grid method to work these out (no grids to help this time):

1. 751 × 4 = **2.** 332 × 6 =

3. 663 × 3 = **4.** 456 × 5 =

5. 843 × 8 =

c) Now extend your grid to work out the following:

1. 35 × 29 =

2. 74 × 41 =

3. 34 × 67 =

Gold

a) Copy and complete:

1. 26 × 55 =

2. 42 × 46 =

3. 66 × 37 =

4. 84 × 54 =

5. 95 × 73 =

b) Use the grid method to work these out (no grids to help this time):

1. 71 × 43 =

2. 82 × 69 =

3. 63 × 38 =

4. 56 × 57 =

5. 84 × 48 =

c) Now extend your grid to work out the following:

1. 352 × 293 =

2. 438 × 170 =

3. 744 × 419 =

4. 235 × 382 =

5. 346 × 677 =

Training Tips

Key words for multiplication are: times, lots of, product, factor, multiply.

Check your answer by approximating or carrying out the reverse operation.

Long multiplication

The standard method for multiplication is called long multiplication.
It is very similar to the grid method – you still need to partition – but it is set out differently.
Look at these two examples:

```
1.    34                          2.    22
    × 18                              × 45
    ‾‾‾‾                              ‾‾‾‾
    340    (34 × 10)                  880    (22 × 40)
    272    (34 × 8)                   110    (22 × 5)
    ‾‾‾‾                              ‾‾‾‾
    612                              990
```

Bronze

a) Copy and complete:

1.
```
    6
  × 12
  ‾‾‾‾
         (6 × 10)
  ‾‾‾‾   (6 × 2)
```

2.
```
    4
  × 13
  ‾‾‾‾
         (4 × 10)
         (4 × 3)
  ‾‾‾‾
```

3.
```
    5
  × 14
  ‾‾‾‾
         (5 × 10)
         (5 × 4)
  ‾‾‾‾
```

b) Work out:

1. 3 × 13 =   **2.** 6 × 15 =

3. 4 × 16 =   **4.** 5 × 14 =

5. 9 × 12 =   **6.** 3 × 18 =

7. 6 × 14 =   **8.** 4 × 17 =

9. 5 × 19 =   **10.** 7 × 13 =

Silver

a) Copy and complete:

1.
```
    24
  × 12
  ‾‾‾‾
         (24 × 10)
  ‾‾‾‾   (24 × 2)
```

2.
```
    17
  × 13
  ‾‾‾‾
         (17 × 10)
  ‾‾‾‾   (17 × 3)
```

3.
```
    29
  × 14
  ‾‾‾‾
         (29 × 10)
  ‾‾‾‾   (29 × 4)
```

b) Work out:

1. 53   **2.** 19   **3.** 23
   ×11   ×16   ×18

4. 25   **5.** 41   **6.** 52
   ×32   ×24   ×43

7. 63   **8.** 15   **9.** 64
   ×45   ×54   ×53

Gold

a) Copy and complete:

1. 324
```
  × 12
  ‾‾‾‾
         (324 × 10)
  ‾‾‾‾   (324 × 2)
```

2. 517
```
  × 13
  ‾‾‾‾
         (517 × 10)
  ‾‾‾‾   (517 × 3)
```

3. 429
```
  × 14
  ‾‾‾‾
         (429 × 10)
  ‾‾‾‾   (429 × 4)
```

b) Work out:

1. 523   **2.** 189   **3.** 283
   ×11   ×16   ×18

4. 225   **5.** 461   **6.** 582
   ×32   ×24   ×43

7. 463   **8.** 715   **9.** 564
   ×45   ×54   ×53

Training Tips

As you gain confidence with this method, you don't need to write the sums in the brackets.

Remember the rules of multiplying by 10.
Check by approximating.

Multiplying decimals

You can use any written method for multiplication when you are multiplying decimals.
You may want to use partitioning.

Example
$5.3 \times 6 = (5 \times 6) + (0.3 \times 6)$
$\qquad = 30 + 1.8$
$\qquad = 31.8$

Bronze

a) Multiply by 2:
1. 1.2
2. 2.1
3. 2.6
4. 4.2
5. 5.3

b) Multiply by 3:
1. 2.3
2. 1.6
3. 4.2
4. 1.1
5. 3.2

c) Multiply by 10:
1. 4.8
2. 5.9
3. 2.5
4. 7.8
5. 9.6

Silver

a) Multiply by 4:
1. 4.6
2. 3.8
3. 6.2
4. 5.7
5. 1.9

b) Multiply by 5:
1. 7.4
2. 8.2
3. 4.8
4. 5.1
5. 6.3

c) Multiply by 100:
1. 3.7
2. 4.2
3. 12.8
4. 16.9
5. 13.4

Gold

a) Multiply by 2:
1. 1.34
2. 4.26
3. 7.54
4. 5.25
5. 1.66

b) Multiply by 3:
1. 1.42
2. 3.25
3. 4.37
4. 2.81
5. 3.98

c) Write the missing number:
1. $1.23 \times \square = 2.46$
2. $5.23 \times \square = 15.69$
3. $7.11 \times \square = 63.99$
4. $0.58 \times \square = 2.32$
5. $5.52 \times \square = 22.08$

Training Tips

Check your answer by adding
$(3.4 \times 3 = 3.4 + 3.4 + 3.4 = 10.2)$

Practise reading decimals out loud.

Short division

The standard method for division is called short division. It uses a sign like this $\overline{)}$ to mean divide.

> *Example*
> The sum $145 \div 3$ is written like this $3\overline{)145}$

You can solve this in the same way as short division – see Example 1.
Your teacher may teach you a different way to solve it – see Example 2.

Example 1	*Example 2*
$3\overline{)145}$	$\qquad$ 48 r1
$\underline{-\ 120}$ (40 x 3)	$3\overline{)\ 145}$
$\quad$ 25	$\qquad$ 12
$\underline{-\ 24}$ (8 x 3)	$\qquad$ 25
$\qquad$ 1	$\qquad$ 24
Answer 48 r 1	$\qquad$ 1
	Answer 48 r 1

 Bronze

a) Practise using short division by answering these questions:

1. $2\overline{)428}$ =   *2.* $3\overline{)369}$ =

3. $2\overline{)728}$ =   *4.* $3\overline{)309}$ =

5. $4\overline{)910}$ =   *6.* $4\overline{)448}$ =

7. $5\overline{)506}$ =   *8.* $5\overline{)327}$ =

9. $4\overline{)257}$ =   *10.* $3\overline{)236}$ =

b) Divide by 2 using short division:

1. £2.16   *2.* £6.46

3. £5.42   *4.* £7.98

5. £3.22

 Silver

a) Practise using short division by answering these questions:

1. $4\overline{)123}$ =   *2.* $5\overline{)133}$ =

3. $6\overline{)135}$ =   *4.* $5\overline{)234}$ =

5. $6\overline{)193}$ =   *6.* $7\overline{)340}$ =

7. $8\overline{)549}$ =   *8.* $8\overline{)341}$ =

9. $9\overline{)512}$ =   *10.* $7\overline{)471}$ =

b) Divide by 3 using short division:

1. £9.33   *2.* £4.26

3. £7.14   *4.* £10.80

5. £2.25

Gold

a) Practise using short division by answering these questions:

1. $8\overline{)5678}$ =   *2.* $6\overline{)2257}$ =

3. $9\overline{)1234}$ =   *4.* $7\overline{)3173}$ =

5. $11\overline{)3687}$ =

b) Work out:

1. $2\overline{)4.85}$ =   *2.* $3\overline{)4.35}$ =

3. $8\overline{)5.71}$ =   *4.* $7\overline{)2.35}$ =

5. $9\overline{)9.12}$ =

c) Divide using short division:

1. $7\overline{)£7.14}$ =   *2.* $6\overline{)£7.38}$ =

3. $9\overline{)£3.24}$ =   *4.* $8\overline{)£8.96}$ =

5. $6\overline{)£6.66}$ =

 Training Tips

 If there is a remainder you can just write r.

 All these words mean division – share, divide, group.

Using a calculator

Using a calculator can help us but we need to be able to understand the answers it gives.

Negative numbers
Your calculator will show negative numbers as -3

More than one step
If a question has brackets in it you must **work out the brackets first** using your calculator, write it down and then finish working out the sum.

Money
When using your calculator to solve money problems you must make sure you understand the answer.

£3.35 − £1.64 =
We type 3.35 − 1.64 = 1.71
The answer is £1.71

Bronze

a) Use your calculator to work out these sums. Be careful – the answers might be negative numbers!

1. 9 − 11 =   **2.** 32 − 74 =
3. 42 − 84 =   **4.** 72 − 34 =

b) Use your calculator to solve these money problems:

1. £4.25 − £3. 14 =
2. £7.34 − £5.82 =
3. £9.73 − £4.26 =
4. £12.45 − £6.55 =
5. £4.70 − £1.34 =

c) Use your calculator to answer these two-step problems. Work out the brackets first.

1. 2 × (23+13) =
2. 23 + (45−23) =
3. 99 − (3 × 6) =

Silver

a) Use your calculator to work out these sums:

1. 139 − 211 =
2. 732 − 574 =
3. 842 − 1184 =
4. 372 − 734 =
5. 465 − 391 =

b) Use your calculator to solve these money problems:

1. £4.24 − £3. 14 =
2. £7.34 − 80p =
3. £9.73 − 45p =
4. £12.45 − 180p =
5. £124.78 − £61.48 =

c) Use your calculator to answer these two-step problems:

1. 6 × (43+83) =
2. 23 + (545−73) =
3. (13×6) − 47 =

Gold

a) Use your calculator to work out these sums:

1. 1369 − 2411 =
2. 7382 − 5474 =
3. 8442 − 4184 =
4. 3742 − 7354 =
5. 4645 − 3591 =

b) Use your calculator to solve these money problems:

1. £4.65 − £2.85 = □
2. £6.54 − □ = 120p
3. £3.73 − □ = 80p
4. £64.75 − □ = £31.50
5. □ − £8.11 = £2.56

c) Use your calculator to answer these two-step problems:

1. (2×4) + (73+53) =
2. (23+12) + (458−53) =
3. (199+23) − (13×7) =

 **Training Tips**

 £1.70 on a calculator will look like 1.7. The calculator will not show the zero.

Don't use a calculator when you could use your brain!

Checking results of calculations

It is important that we check our answers to make sure they make sense and that we have not made a mistake. Over the next two pages you will practise this skill.

Check with the inverse operation when using a calculator

When you are using a calculator to work out sums, check you have got the right answer by putting in the inverse operation.

If you have worked out $345 \times 32 = 11040$

check this is correct by typing in

$11040 \div 32 = 345$
You were correct.

Check the sum of several numbers by adding in a different order

If you have to add several numbers together, then adding them in a different order is a good way to check you have not made a mistake:

> *Example*
> $8 + 9 + 7 + 4 = 28$
> Different order: $7 + 8 + 4 + 9 = 28$
> As it is the same answer you can assume it is correct.

Check with an equivalent sum

If you have worked out $34 + 39 = 73$
check by working out an equivalent sum:

> *Example*
> * $34 + 30 + 9 =$
> * Double $34 + 5 =$
> * $34 + 40 - 1 =$ etc.

Checking results of calculations

Bronze

Silver

Gold

a) Check the following sums using your calculator. Mark them right or wrong.

1. 35 × 76 = 2660

2. 456 + 753 = 1208

3. 987 − 379 = 609

4. 254 ÷ 2 = 128

5. 8664 + 1245 = 9909

b) Add up these sums and then check by adding them in a different order:

1. 9 + 4 + 5 =

2. 5 + 3 + 6 =

3. 8 + 7 + 4 =

4. 2 + 9 + 5 =

5. 3 + 8 + 7 =

c) Work out these sums and the equivalent calculation:

1. 24 + 25 = (24×2) + 1 =

2. 13 + 29 = (13+30) − 1 =

3. 25 + 62 = 25 + 60 + 2 =

4. 8 × 12 = (8×10) + 16 =

5. 68 − 34 = (68−30) − 4 =

a) Using your calculator, copy and complete these sums:

1. □ + 345 = 685

2. 456 − □ = 103

3. 45 × □ = 585

4. 1568 ÷ 28 = □

5. □ ÷ 369 = 12

b) Add up these sums and then check by adding them in a different order:

1. 11 + 12 + 6 + 5 =

2. 9 + 5 + 12 + 13 =

3. 25 + 12 + 9 + 8 =

4. 16 + 9 + 18 + 3 =

5. 37 + 9 + 5 + 6 =

c) Work out these sums and the equivalent calculation:

1. 125 + 126 =

2. 654 + 199 =

3. 563 − 21 =

4. 982 − 125 =

5. 56 × 11 =

a) Using your calculator, copy and complete these sums:

1. □ + 56.34 = 89.53

2. 67.45 − □ = 12.09

3. 678 × □ = 155.94

4. 8429 ÷ □ = 42145

5. □ ÷ 0.47 = 358

b) Add up these sums and then check by adding them in a different order:

1. 0.23 + 0.36 + 0.3 + 0.2 =

2. 0.58 + 0.12 + 0.04 + 0.03 =

3. 145 + 12 + 11 + 15 =

4. 482 + 26 + 14 + 22 =

5. 265 + 110 + 124 + 201 =

c) Work out these sums and the equivalent calculation:

1. 1236 + 1238 =

2. 5689 + 1999 =

3. 5698 − 2566 =

4. 12.36 − 6.98 =

5. 2585 × 16 =

Training Tips

You should check every sum you work out to avoid mistakes.

Checking sums:
• Change the order to check.
• Do an equivalent sum.

Checking results by approximating

Another way to check your answers is to approximate. That means to round the numbers in the sum to the nearest 10, 100 or 1000 so that you know roughly what the answer should look like.

Example

19×21 round both numbers ⟶ $20 \times 20 = 400$.
400 is the approximate answer.
When we carry out the actual operation we know the answer should be around 400.

 **Bronze**

 Silver

 **Gold**

Bronze	Silver	Gold
a) Round these numbers to the nearest 10:	**a) Round these numbers to the nearest 100:**	**a) Round these numbers to the nearest 1000:**
1. 62 *2.* 16 *3.* 92	*1.* 282 *2.* 817 *3.* 307	*1.* 6282 *2.* 8175 *3.* 3507
4. 48 *5.* 25	*4.* 530 *5.* 845	*4.* 7530 *5.* 4845
b) Estimate the answer by rounding each number to its nearest 10 and then adding:	**b) Estimate the answer by rounding each number to its nearest 10 or 100 and then adding:**	**b) Estimate the answer by rounding each number to its nearest 100 or 1000 and then adding:**
1. 19 + 21 =	*1.* 108 + 21 =	*1.* 1908 + 201 =
2. 43 + 32 =	*2.* 213 + 19 =	*2.* 2713 + 419 =
3. 51 + 42 =	*3.* 168 + 19 =	*3.* 4168 + 619 =
4. 37 + 22 =	*4.* 314 + 28 =	*4.* 8314 + 728 =
5. 53 + 16 =	*5.* 320 + 42 =	*5.* 3320 + 142 =
c) Estimate the answer by rounding each number to its nearest 10 and then multiplying:	**c) Estimate the answer by rounding each number to its nearest 10 or 100 and then multiplying:**	**c) Estimate the answer by rounding each number to its nearest 100 or 1000 and then multiplying:**
1. $28 \times 39 =$	*1.* $382 \times 18 =$	*1.* $1382 \times 180 =$
2. $11 \times 35 =$	*2.* $431 \times 21 =$	*2.* $2431 \times 210 =$
3. $31 \times 27 =$	*3.* $410 \times 23 =$	*3.* $3410 \times 230 =$
4. $18 \times 23 =$	*4.* $472 \times 22 =$	*4.* $6472 \times 220 =$
5. $29 \times 41 =$	*5.* $123 \times 48 =$	*5.* $8123 \times 480 =$

 **Training Tips**

 Round digits less than 5 down.

 Round digits 5 or more up.

Length

We use the following measurements to measure **length**.

mm = millimetres	cm = centimetres	m = metres	km = kilometres
1km = 1000m	1m = 100cm	1m = 1000mm	1cm = 10mm

Use these facts to help you answer the questions.

Bronze

a) **Convert these measurements:**

1. 6m = ☐ cm
2. 9m = ☐ cm
3. 7m = ☐ mm
4. 4cm = ☐ mm
5. 8km = ☐ m

b) **Suggest suitable units for these:**

1. Length of an ant
2. Distance from London to Scotland
3. Length of a classroom
4. Length of a paper clip
5. Height of school building

c) **Measure these lines in cm:**

1. ————————
2. ———————————
3. ———
4. ——————————
5. —————

Silver

a) **Convert these measurements:**

1. 17m = ☐ cm
2. 27m = ☐ cm
3. 64m = ☐ mm
4. 120km = ☐ m
5. 624cm = ☐ mm

b) **Suggest suitable units for these:**

1. Width of your book
2. Length of school hall
3. The distance from Scotland to Wales
4. Length of a fly
5. Length of River Thames

c) **Measure these lines in mm:**

1. ——
2. —————
3. ————
4. ————
5. —————

Gold

a) **Convert these measurements:**

1. 2000cm = ☐ m
2. 1500mm = ☐ cm
3. 25000m = ☐ km
4. 50000mm = ☐ m
5. 48000cm = ☐ m

b) **Suggest suitable units for these:**

1. Distance from England to Africa
2. Length of a CD box
3. Length of a pin
4. Length of a running track
5. Distance travelled by a car

c) **Measure these lines in mm:**

1. ——————————
2. —————
3. ———————————
4. ——————————
5. ———————————

Training Tips

Remember: × 10 digits move one place to the left.

Try to picture what 1 mm, 1 cm, 1 mm and 1 km look like.

Mass

When we weigh objects we find their **mass**.

1 kilogram (kg) = 1000 grams (g)
6 kg = (6 x 1000) = 6000 g

Bronze

a) Copy and complete:

1. 4 kg = ☐ g
2. 2 kg = ☐ g
3. 23 kg = ☐ g
4. 36 kg = ☐ g
5. 52 kg = ☐ g
6. 163 kg = ☐ g
7. 284 kg = ☐ g
8. 5000 g = ☐ kg
9. 3000 g = ☐ kg
10. 9000 g = ☐ kg

b) Suggest suitable units for the mass of:

1. An egg
2. A person
3. An elephant
4. A paper clip
5. A boot

Silver

a) Convert the following to grams:

1. 8 kg = ☐ g
2. 29 kg = ☐ g
3. 3.263 kg = ☐ g
4. 8.941 kg = ☐ g
5. 26.31 kg = ☐ g

b) Convert the following to kg:

1. 7000 g = ☐ kg
2. 23000 g = ☐ kg
3. 6730 g = ☐ kg
4. 9800 g = ☐ kg
5. 42830 g = ☐ kg

c) Suggest suitable units for the mass of:

1. A carrot
2. A car
3. A man
4. A slipper
5. A torch

Gold

a) Convert the following to grams:

1. 3.2 kg = ☐ g
2. 0.086 kg = ☐ g
3. 0.321 kg = ☐ g
4. 6.28 kg = ☐ g
5. 9.04 kg = ☐ g

b) Convert the following to kg:

1. 1682 g = ☐ kg
2. 9324 g = ☐ kg
3. 600 g = ☐ kg
4. 872 g = ☐ kg
5. 94 g = ☐ kg

c) Suggest suitable units for the mass of:

1. A CD case
2. A motorbike
3. A boat
4. A model airplane
5. A caravan

Training Tips

 × 1000 digit moves 3 places to the left and ÷ 1000 digit moves 3 places to the right.

 kg = kilogram
g = gram

Capacity

Measures of **capacity** are normally used for liquids.

1 litre (l) = 1000 millilitres (ml)

Bronze

a) Convert to ml:

1. 6l

2. 12l

3. 8l

4. 27l

5. 36l

b) Convert to litres:

1. 8000 ml

2. 12000 ml

3. 4000 ml

4. 5000 ml

5. 26000 ml

c) Suggest suitable units to measure the following capacities:

1. A fish tank

2. A cup of water

3. A lake

4. A kettle

5. A spoonful of medicine

Silver

a) Convert to ml:

1. 36l

2. 6.30l

3. 27.40l

4. 89.36l

5. 7.04l

b) Convert to litres:

1. 7000 ml

2. 6000 ml

3. 620 ml

4. 8940 ml

5. 3621 ml

c) Suggest suitable units to measure the following capacities:

1. A swimming pool

2. A bowl of water

3. A petrol tank in a car

4. A bottle of perfume

5. An eggcup

Gold

a) Convert to ml:

1. 0.043l

2. 0.621l

3. 0.4l

4. 3.62l

5. 7.03l

b) Convert to litres:

1. 3670 ml

2. 1498 ml

3. 270 ml

4. 46 ml

5. 824 ml

c) Suggest suitable units to measure the following capacities:

1. A bath

2. A pond

3. A jug of water

4. A teaspoon

5. A sink

Training Tips

× 1000 digit moves 3 places to the left and ÷ 1000 digit moves 3 places to the right.

ml = millilitre
l = litre

Area

Area is the size of a surface or the amount of space it covers.

Using squares can help work out the area of shapes.
The area of this shape is 8 squares.

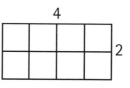

For a rectangle, you can also use this rule:

Area = Length x Breadth

Bronze

a) **Work out the areas of these shapes by counting squares:**

1. 5, 2

2. 3, 4, 2

3. 6, 1, 2, 2

b) **Work out the areas of the following using the rule:**

1. 4, 2

2. 5, 3

3. 3, 2

4. 6, 3

c) **Draw a shape with an area of:**

1. 12 squares **2.** 24 squares

3. 6 squares **4.** 17 squares

5. 32 squares

Silver

a) **Work out the areas of the following using the rule:**

1. 6 cm, 5 cm

2. 4 mm, 9 mm

3. 10 km, 6 km

b) **Measure these rectangles in mm and work out their area:**

1.

2.

3.

c) **Draw a shape on cm² paper with an area of:**

1. 26 cm² **2.** 19 cm²

3. 43 cm² **4.** 34 cm²

5. 27 cm²

Gold

a) **Work out the areas of these shapes:**

1. 11, 9, 3, 2

2. 27, 4, 8, 2

3. 15, 6, 2, 5

b) **Measure these rectangles, to the nearest mm, and find the area:**

1.

2.

3.

4.

c) **Draw a shape on cm² paper with an area of:**

1. 140 mm² **2.** 23 mm²

3. 270 mm² **4.** 64 mm²

5. 390 mm²

Training Tips

Remember the rule:
Area = Length x Breadth

Remember to check units,
mm², cm², m², km²

Perimeter

Perimeter is the distance around the outside of a closed shape.

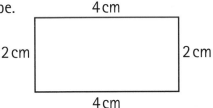

Example

Perimeter = 4 cm + 2 cm + 4 cm + 2 cm
= 12 cm

Bronze

a) **Work out the perimeters of these shapes:**

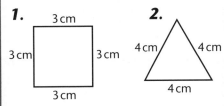

1. 3 cm / 3 cm / 3 cm / 3 cm

2. 4 cm / 4 cm / 4 cm

3. 4 cm / 6 cm / 3 cm / 5 cm

b) **Measure the sides of these shapes in cm and find the perimeter:**

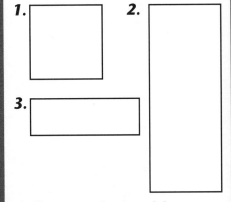

1. **2.** **3.**

c) **Draw a shape with perimeter of:**

1. 8 cm **2.** 12 cm **3.** 24 cm

4. 19 cm **5.** 32 cm

Silver

a) **Work out the perimeters of these shapes:**

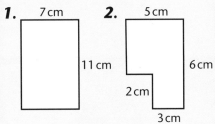

1. 7 cm / 11 cm

2. 5 cm / 6 cm / 2 cm / 3 cm

3. 6 cm / 2 cm / 8 cm / 3 cm / 7 cm / 12 cm

b) **Measure the perimeters of these shapes to the nearest cm:**

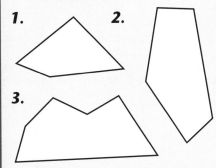

1. **2.** **3.**

c) **Draw an irregular shape with perimeter:**

1. 36 cm **2.** 22.5 cm

3. 19 cm **4.** 32.5 cm

5. 48 cm

Gold

a) **Find the perimeter of:**

1. A regular pentagon with sides 8 cm

2. A regular octagon with sides 7 cm

3. A square with sides 12 mm

4. A regular decagon with sides 13 cm

5. A regular hexagon with sides 9 mm

b) **Measure the perimeters of the following shapes in mm:**

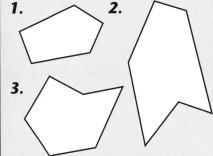

1. **2.** **3.**

c) **Draw a shape with perimeter:**

1. 36 cm **2.** 142 mm

3. 72 cm **4.** 487 mm

5. 48 cm

Training Tips

 A square = all sides are equal.

 Regular shape means all sides have the same length.

Reading from scales

Before trying to read any scales, work out what the scale is telling you.
What are the first and last numbers?

Example

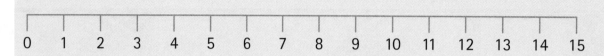

0   1   2   3   4   5   6   7   8   9   10   11   12   13   14   15

This scale is used to measure length.
It measures between 0 and 15 centimetres in units of one centimetre.

a) **Work out what number each letter is pointing to.**

1. A =   *2.* B =   *3.* C =   *4.* D =   *5.* E =

b) **On the vertical scale what number is each letter pointing to?**
1. F =   *2.* G =   *3.* H =   *4.* I =   *5.* J =

c) **What number is each letter pointing to?**

1. K =   *2.* L =   *3.* M =   *4.* N =   *5.* O =

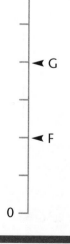

 **Training Tips**

 Work out the scale before you start.

Reading from scales

Silver

a) What number is each letter pointing to?

300   500

1. A =   **2.** B =   **3.** C =   **4.** D =   **5.** E =

b) On the vertical scale what number is each letter pointing to?

1. F =   **2.** G =   **3.** H =   **4.** I =   **5.** J =

c) What number is each letter pointing to?

60   80

1. K =   **2.** L =   **3.** M =   **4.** N =   **5.** O =

Gold

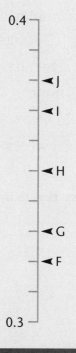

a) What number is each letter pointing to?

14   16

1. A =   **2.** B =   **3.** C =   **4.** D =   **5.** E =

b) On the vertical scale what number is each letter pointing to?

1. F =   **2.** G =   **3.** H =   **4.** I =   **5.** J =

c) What number is each letter pointing to?

2000   4000

1. K =   **2.** L =   **3.** M =   **4.** N =   **5.** O =

Training Tips

You need at least two numbers to work out the scale.

Time

We measure time in a lot of ways:

1 minute = 60 seconds
1 hour = 60 minutes
1 day = 24 hours
1 week = 7 days
1 year = 365 days

When we read the time we can read analogue and digital clocks.

Analogue

Digital

Digital clocks use the 24-hour system.

Any time after 12.00 on a digital clock shows it is a time after midday.

Analogue clocks use am and pm to show if it is the morning or afternoon.

Bronze

a) Copy and complete these times:

1. 2 minutes = ☐ seconds

2. 3 hours = ☐ minutes

3. 2 days = ☐ hours

4. 4 weeks = ☐ hours

5. 1 month = ☐ weeks

b) Write these times in words:

1. 04:23

2. 12:00

3. 13:00

4. 14:12

5. 16:45

c) Use this table to answer the questions:

Blue Peter	5pm	5.30pm
News	5.30pm	6.10pm

1. For how many minutes is Blue Peter on?

2. For how many minutes is Transformers on?

3. If I watch the News and Transformers, how long will I be watching TV?

4. If Transformers lasted for 1 hour, when would it finish?

Training Tips

 am – ante meridian

 pm – post meridian

Time

Silver

a) Copy and complete:

1. 6 minutes = ☐ seconds

2. 5 hours = ☐ minutes

3. 6 days = ☐ hours

4. 8 weeks = ☐ days

5. 2 years = ☐ days

b) Write the following times in digital:

1.   **2.**

3.   **4.**

c) Use this table to answer the questions:

School	12.30	13.01	13.32	14.03
Hospital	12.35	13.06	13.37	14.08
Shops	12.42	13.13	13.44	14.15
Station	12.53	13.24	13.55	14.26

1. How long does the journey take from the School to the Shops?

2. How long does the journey take from the Hospital to the Station?

3. If the bus leaves the Hospital at 14.08, what time will it reach the Station?

4. A bus arrives at the Shops at 13.13. What time did it leave the School?

Gold

a) Copy and complete:

1. 300 seconds = ☐ minutes

2. 420 minutes = ☐ hours

3. 63 days = ☐ weeks

4. 216 hours = ☐ days

5. 1095 days = ☐ years

b) Write the times shown below in digital and words:

1.   **2.**   **3.**

c) Use this train timetable to answer the questions:

London Victoria	07:42	———	09:25	11:24
Streatham Hill	09:02	10:09	10:45	12:44
West Norwood	09:12	———	10:55	12:54
Crystal Palace	09:22	———	11:05	13:04
West Croydon	09:37	10:44	11:20	13:19

1. How long does the journey take from London Victoria to West Norwood?

2. How long does the journey take from Streatham Hill to West Croydon?

3. If I need to be in West Croydon for 11:00, what time train should I catch from West Norwood?

4. If I arrive at Crystal Palace at 1.04pm, what time train did I catch from Streatham Hill?

2-D shapes

2-D shapes have corners and sides.

These are some 2-D shapes:

There are four different types of triangle:

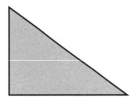

Right-angled triangle
– It has a right angle (90°)

Equilateral triangle
- Has 3 sides that are equal
- Has 3 angles that are equal

Isosceles triangle
- 2 sides are equal length
- 2 equal angles

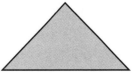

Scalene triangle
- No sides are equal
- No equal angles

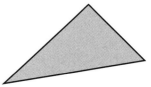

Bronze

a) Decide which type of triangles these are:

1.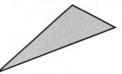

2.

3.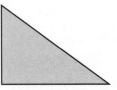

4.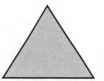

5.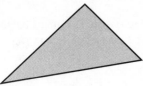

6.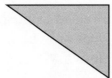

b) Name the following shapes:

1.

2.

3.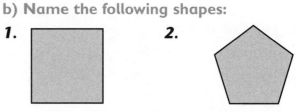

4.

5.

c) Write a description of each of the shapes above.

2-D shapes

Silver

a) Name each triangle:

1.

2.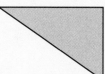

3.

4.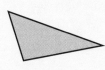

5.

6.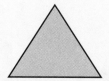

b) Name the following shapes:

1.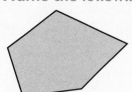

2.

3.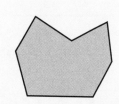

4.

c) For each shape above, describe the shape's properties.

Gold

a) Draw the following shapes:

1. A right-angled scalene triangle
2. An equilateral triangle
3. A non right-angled isosceles triangle
4. A right-angled isosceles triangle
5. A non right-angled scalene triangle

b) Draw the following shapes:

1. Trapezium
2. Parallelogram
3. Rhombus
4. Decagon
5. Heptagon

c) Name these shapes:

1. This shape has four right angles and all its sides are equal
2. This shape has only one pair of parallel sides
3. This shape has two pairs of parallel sides and no right angles
4. This shape has four right angles and two pairs of parallel lines
5. This shape has all sides the same length and has a diamond shape

Training Tips

 Use a ruler when drawing shapes.

 Right angle = 90°

3-D shapes

3-D shapes have faces, edges and vertices.

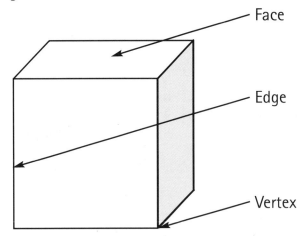

Face

Edge

Vertex

1.

2.

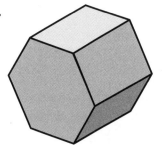

3.

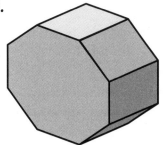

4.

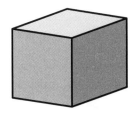

5.

6.

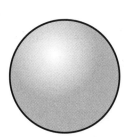

7.

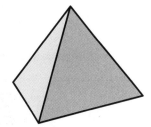

8.

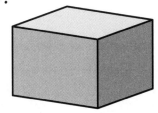

9.

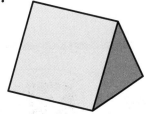

3-D shapes

Bronze

Name all 15 shapes.

Silver

Name each shape and say how many vertices, edges and faces each has.

Gold

For each shape, give:

- its name
- the shapes of all the faces
- the number of vertices, edges and faces

10.

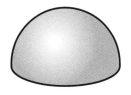

11.

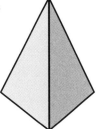

12.

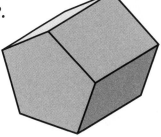

13.

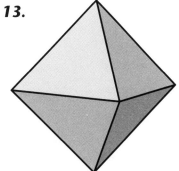

14.

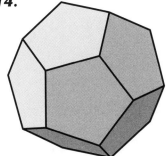

15.

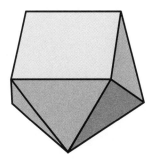

 **Training Tips**

 3-D = three-dimensional

 One vertex, two or more vertices.

Visualise 3-D shapes

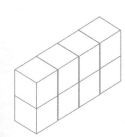

Look at this drawing of a 3-D shape. How many cubes are needed to make it?

The answer is 8.

On this page you are going to practise visualising 3-D shapes from drawings.

A

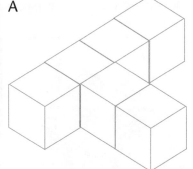

B

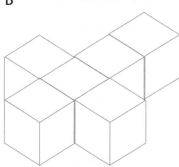

C

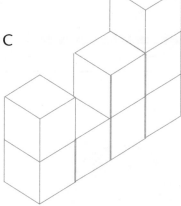

D

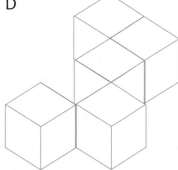

E

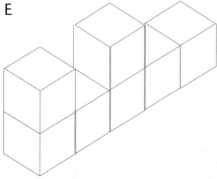

a) How many cubes are there in these shapes?

1. A =   *2.* B =   *3.* C =

4. D =   *5.* E =

b) What is the least number of unit cubes needed to make the shapes into cuboids?

1. A =   *2.* B =   *3.* C =

4. D =   *5.* E =

c) What is the least number of unit cubes needed to make the shapes into cubes?

1. A =   *2.* B =   *3.* C =

4. D =   *5.* E =

 **Training Tips**

Try to visualise the cubes.

Be careful not to count cubes twice.

Visualise 3-D shapes

A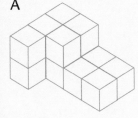

C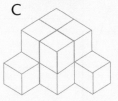

E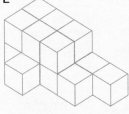

B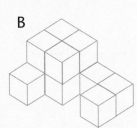

D

a) How many cubes are there in these shapes?

1. A =   **2.** B =   **3.** C =

4. D =   **5.** E =

b) What is the least number of unit cubes needed to make the shapes into cuboids?

1. A =   **2.** B =   **3.** C =

4. D =   **5.** E =

c) What is the least number of unit cubes needed to make the shapes into cubes?

1. A =   **2.** B =   **3.** C =

4. D =   **5.** E =

Gold

A, B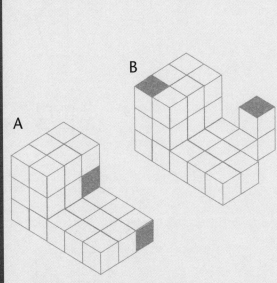

C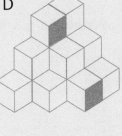

D, E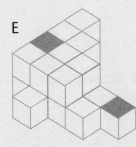

a) How many cubes are there in these shapes?

1. A =   **2.** B =   **3.** C =

4. D =   **5.** E =

b) How many cubes are needed to make the shapes into cuboids?

1. A =   **2.** B =   **3.** C =

4. D =   **5.** E =

c) What is the least number of unit cubes needed to cover and join the two shaded faces?

1. A =   **2.** B =   **3.** C =

4. D =   **5.** E =

Symmetry

Symmetry means a shape where two halves are a mirror image of each other.

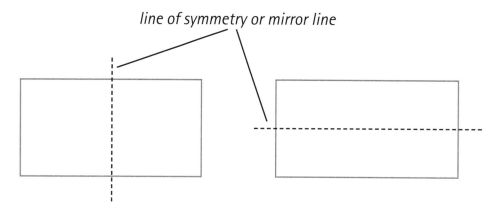

line of symmetry or mirror line

A rectangle has two lines of symmetry.
There are two places you could place a mirror to get an exact image of the rectangle.
You may find that using a small mirror can help in these questions.

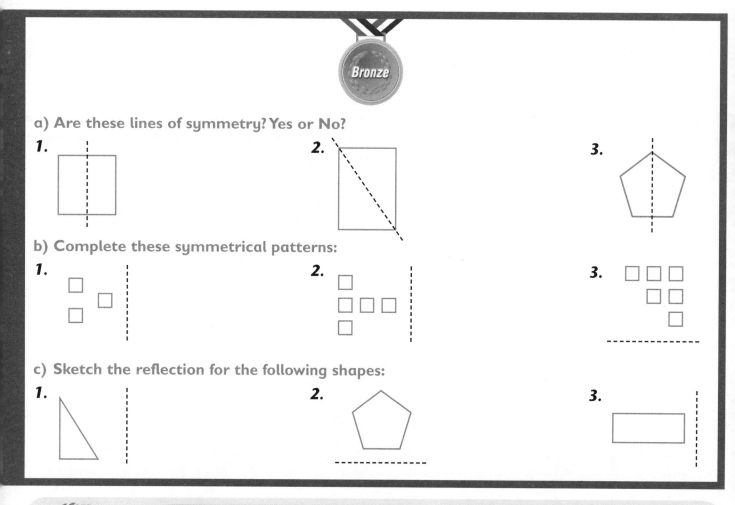

Bronze

a) Are these lines of symmetry? Yes or No?

1. **2.** **3.**

b) Complete these symmetrical patterns:

1. **2.** **3.**

c) Sketch the reflection for the following shapes:

1. **2.** **3.**

 Training Tips

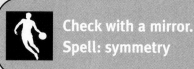 Check with a mirror.
Spell: **symmetry**

 You can also check by cutting
out a shape and folding it up.

Symmetry

Silver

a) How many lines of symmetry are there in each shape?

1.

2.

3.

b) Complete these symmetrical patterns:

1.

2.

3.

c) Sketch the reflection of these:

1.

2.

3.

Gold

a) Draw a shape with:

1. One line of symmetry
2. Two lines of symmetry
3. Three lines of symmetry
4. Four lines of symmetry
5. No lines of symmetry

b) Complete these symmetrical patterns in all four quadrants:

1.

2.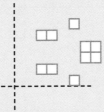

3.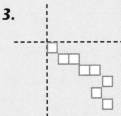

c) Sketch reflections for the following:

1.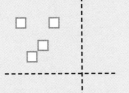

2.

3.

Nets

A net of a shape is a solid shape folded out flat.

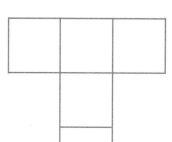

Bronze

Can you make a cube out of these nets? Draw and cut them out to help.

1.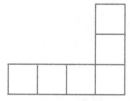

2.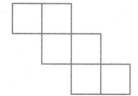

3.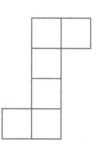

4.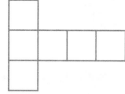

5.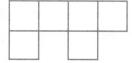

6.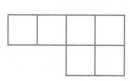

7.

8.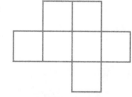

9.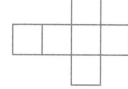

10.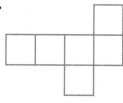

Training Tips

Cutting out the nets and testing may help.

Try to visualise folding the net.

Nets

Silver

a) Decide which of these are nets for a cuboid:

1.

2.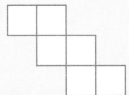

3.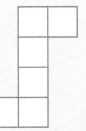

4.

5.

b) Complete these nets to make a cube:

1.

2.

3.

4.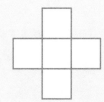

5.

Gold

a) Can you make a cuboid from these nets?

1.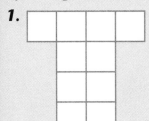

2.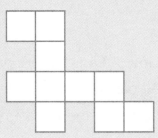

3.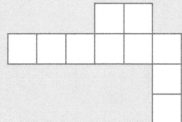

4.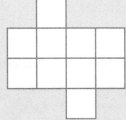

5.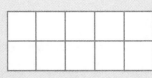

b) Draw a net of:

1. A square-based pyramid

2. A triangular prism

3. A tetrahedron

4. A hexagonal prism

5. A pentagonal prism

Perpendicular and parallel lines

Perpendicular lines – cross at right angles.

Example

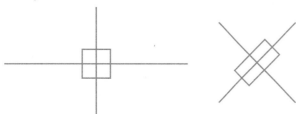

Parallel lines – are lines that go in the same direction and never cross.

Example

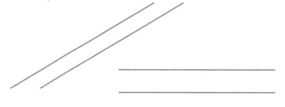

Bronze

a) How many pairs of parallel lines can you see in these shapes?

1.   *2.*  *3.*   *4.*   *5.*

b) How many perpendicular lines can you see in these shapes?

1.   *2.*   *3.*   *4.*   *5.*

c) True or false?

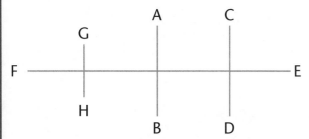

1. Lines AB and CD are parallel

2. All parallel lines cross each other

3. Lines GH and CD are parallel

4. Lines EF and CD are perpendicular

5. Lines AB and GH are perpendicular

Training Tips

 Make sure you can spell perpendicular and parallel.

 Look out for the different lines.

Perpendicular and parallel lines

Silver

a) How many pairs of parallel lines can you see in these diagrams?

1. 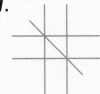   **2.**    **3.**    **4.**    **5.**

b) How many pairs of perpendicular lines can you see in the diagrams above?

c) True or false?

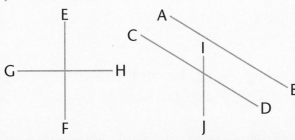

1. GH and IJ are parallel

2. EF and IJ are parallel

3. EF and GH are perpendicular

4. Perpendicular lines always cross each other

5. AB and CD are parallel

Gold

a) Draw the following shapes:

1. An octagon with only 3 pairs of parallel lines

2. An octagon with 4 pairs of perpendicular lines

3. A decagon with 4 pairs of parallel lines

4. A pentagon with no parallel or perpendicular lines

5. An octagon with 2 pairs of parallel lines and 2 pairs of perpendicular lines

b) Look at these shapes and describe how many parallel and perpendicular lines there are:

1.

2.

3.

4.

5.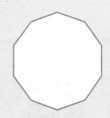

Angles

An angle is a measure of space between two straight lines.

 angle

There are three different types of angle.

Right angle = 90°   Acute angle = angle less than 90°   Obtuse angle = angle more than 90°

We measure angles in degrees (°) using a protractor.
You will need a protractor to answer these questions.

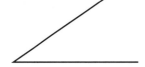 Bronze

a) Identify these angles as acute or obtuse:

1.

2.

3.

4.

b) Estimate these angles:

1.
120° or 150°?

2.
 30° or 60°?

3.
60° or 80°?

4.
 130° or 150°?

c) Measure these angles:

1.

2.

3.

4.

Training Tips

Be careful which scale you use on a protractor.

Look around the room. Can you find an acute or obtuse angle?

Angles

Silver

a) Identify these angles as acute or obtuse:

1.

2.

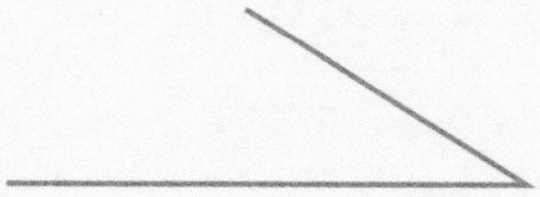

3.

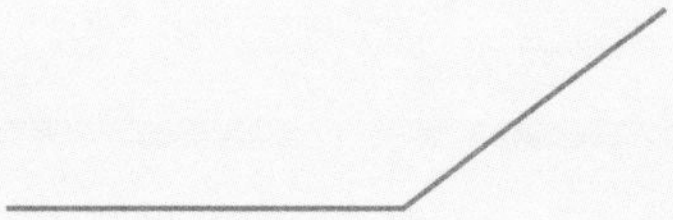

4.

b) Estimate these angles:

1.

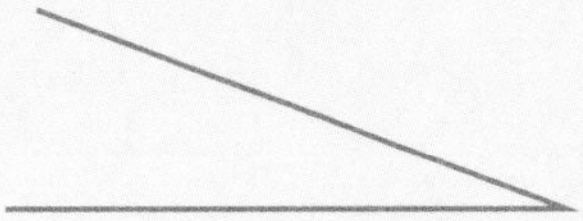

2.

3.

4.

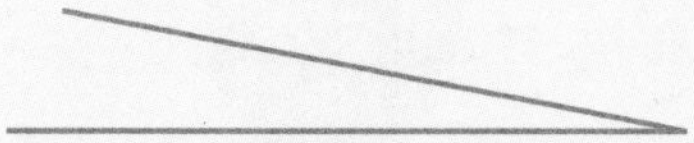

c) Measure these angles:

1.

2.

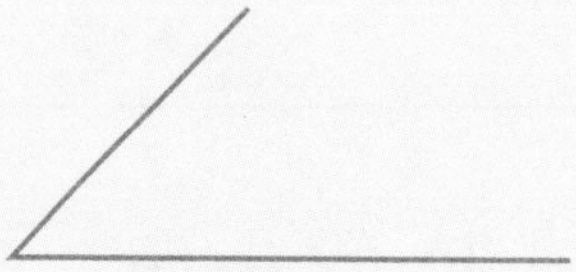

3.

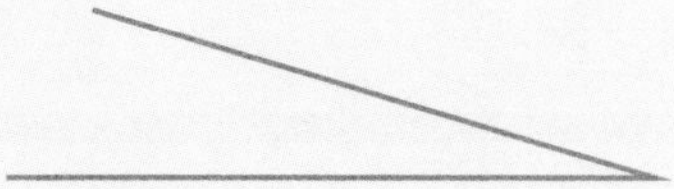

4.

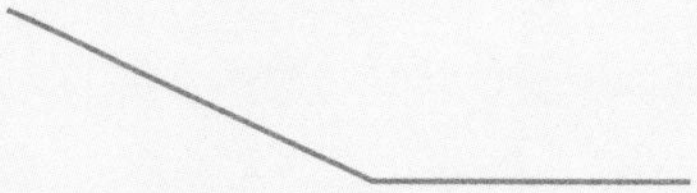

Gold

a) Estimate these angles:

1.

2.

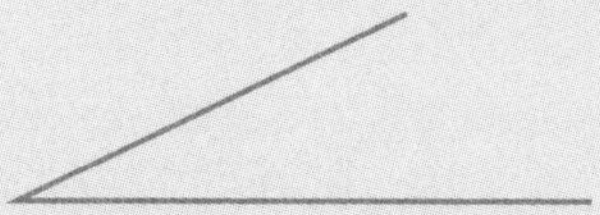

3.

4.

5.

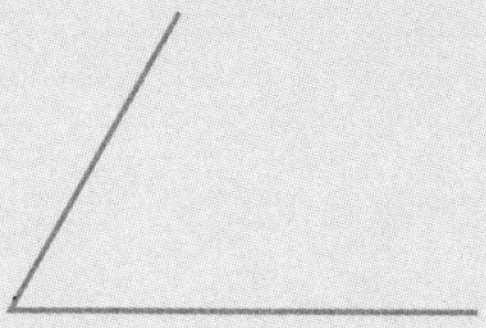

b) Measure these angles:

1.

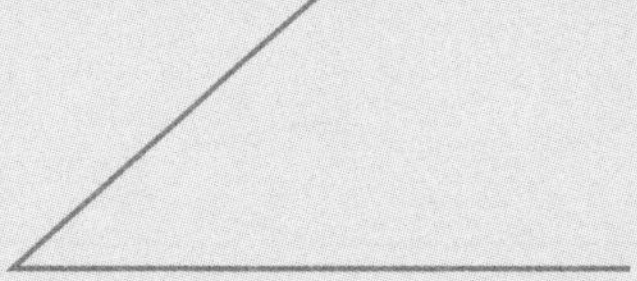

2.

3.

4.

5.

c) Draw these angles:

1. 75°   **2.** 120°   **3.** 325°

4. 150°   **5.** 36°

Angles in a straight line

Half a turn is 180 degrees.
When you draw 180° angle, it is a straight line.

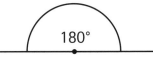

180°

Any angles on a straight line add up to 180°.

The total angles in a circle is 2 x 180° = 360°.

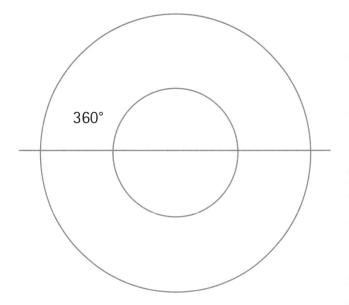

360°

Example

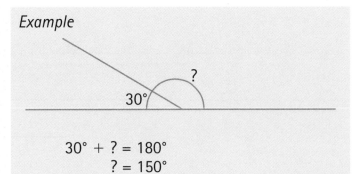

?

30°

$30° + ? = 180°$
$? = 150°$

Bronze

Using the facts you have
learned, work out the
missing angles:

1.

70°   ?

2.

40°   ?

3.

65°   ?

4.

115°   ?

5.

150°

?

6.

170°

?

7.

165°

?

8.

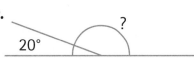

?

15°

9.

175°

?

10.

?

20°

11.

90°   ?

 **Training
Tips**

 **180° = straight line = half turn
360° = circle = whole turn**

**Use a protractor to check the
facts above.**

Angles in a straight line

Silver

a) Using the facts you have learned, work out the missing angles:

1.
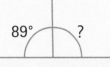
62° ?

2.

89° ?

3.

117° ?

4.

32° ?

5.

71° ?

6.

145° ?

7.

176° ?

b) Now work out these:

1.
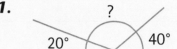
20° ? 40°

2.
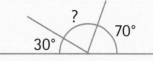
30° ? 70°

3.
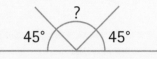
45° ? 45°

4.

100° ? 10°

Gold

a) Find the missing angles:

1.

28° ? 63°

2.

112° ? 27°

3.

12° ? 15°

4.
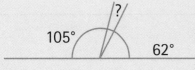
105° ? 62°

b) Find the missing angles:

1.

67° ?

2.

124° ?

3.
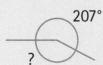
207° ?

4.

54° ?

c) Find the missing angles:

1.
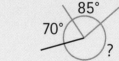
70° 85° ?

2.

110° 95° ?

3.

15° 87° ?

4.
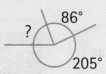
? 86° 205°

Coordinates

Coordinates give you a position on a grid.

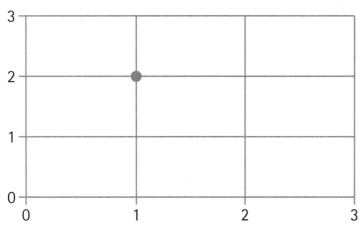

The position of the dot is (1, 2). 1 along and 2 up.

Remember to go ⟶ (along the corridor) and ↑ (up the stairs)

Bronze

a) Draw a 5 x 5 grid. Plot these points on the grid and join them up:

1. (2,2)

2. (2,4)

3. (4,2)

4. (4,4)

5. Name the shape you can see.

b) Draw a new 5 x 5 grid. Plot these points on the grid and join them up:

1. (1,1)

2. (1,3)

3. (5,1)

4. (5,3)

5. Name the shape you can see.

c) Complete the coordinates of each point on the picture:

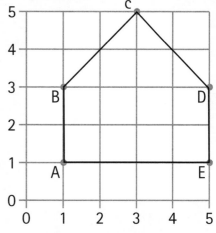

1. A = (1,)   **2.** B = (1,)

3. C = (3,)   **4.** D = (, 3)

5. E = (, 1)

Training Tips

Remember when reading and using coordinates, along first and then up!

You say one axis or two axes. (0, 0) is called the origin.

Coordinates

Silver

a) **Draw a 10 x 10 grid. Plot these points on the grid and join them up:**

1. (1,1), (2,3), (3,1)

2. (1,5), (1,7), (3,7), (3,5)

3. (6,6), (8,6), (9,8), (7,9), (5,8)

4. (7,1), (7,4), (9,4), (9,1)

5. Name these shapes.

b) **Look at this grid. Write down the coordinates of each point:**

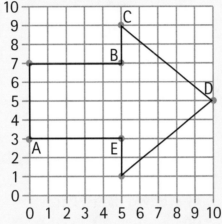

1. A =   **2.** B =   **3.** C =

4. D =   **5.** E =

c) **What extra coordinate will be needed to make a square?**

1. (2,4), (2,7), (5,7), (,)

2. (4,8), (6,8), (4,10), (,)

3. (1,7), (1,12), (6,12), (,)

4. (5,1), (2,1), (5,4), (,)

5. (6,15), (1,10), (6,10), (,)

Gold

a) **Without plotting, predict what shapes these coordinates will make:**

1. (2,1), (4,1), (3,4)

2. (0,0), (2,0), (0,3), (2,3)

3. (13,11), (15,11), (16,13), (14,14), (12,13)

4. (5,4), (4,3), (5,2), (6,2), (7,3), (6,4)

5. (8,6), (3,6), (3,3), (8,3)

b) **Draw this grid in your book:**

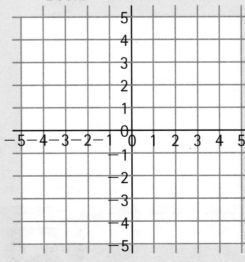

Now plot these points on the grid:

1. (2,2), (2,5), (5,5), (5,2)

2. (−2,2), (−4,2), (−3,4)

3. (−2,−2), (−4,−2), (−5,−4), (−3,−5), (−1,−4)

4. (1,−2), (1,−5), (2,−5), (2,−2)

5. Name these shapes.

Puzzles - what is my number?

Using the clues you are given, you need to find each mystery number.

Example	My number is less than 10.	It could be 0, 1, 2, 3, 4, 5, 6, 7, 8 or 9.
	My number is odd.	It could be 1, 3, 5, 7 or 9.
	It is divisible by 3.	It could be 3 or 9.
	It is a square number.	Answer = 9

 Bronze

 **Silver**

 **Gold**

Bronze

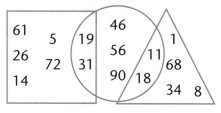

61 5 19 46 1
26 72 31 56 11 68
14 90 18 34 8

1. My number is inside the circle and inside the triangle. It is odd.

2. My number is inside the square but not inside the circle. It can be divided by 7 without a remainder.

3. My number is in the circle and inside the square. It is greater than 20.

4. My number is even. It is inside the triangle. It can be divided exactly by 6.

5. My number is not inside the triangle and not inside the square. It is less than 50.

6. My number is odd. It is divisible by 5. It is in the square.

Silver

Who am I?

1. I have two digits. I am an even number. One of my digits is 2. The sum of my digits is 7.

2. I have two digits. I am greater than 60. I can be divided exactly by 5 and by 7.

3. I have two digits. I am a square number. I am a multiple of 5.

4. I have two digits and I am between 10 and 20. I am a multiple of 3 and the sum of my digits is 3.

5. I am a two-digit even number between 20 and 40. I am in the six times table. The sum of my digits is 6.

6. I have three digits. I can be divided exactly by 3 and 8. I am less than 130.

Gold

Who am I?

1. I am less than 500. I am divisible by 11 and 5. I have three digits. The sum of my digits is 14.

2. I am a four-digit number. I am less than 4900 but more than 3600. I am a square number. I am a multiple of 15 and 5.

3. I am a two-digit odd number less than 100. I am a square number and the sum of my digits is 9.

4. I am the smallest number that leaves a remainder of 3 when divided by 7.

5. I have three digits. My hundreds digit is 5 greater than my tens digit. I am a multiple of 7. One of my digits is 5 but I am not divisible by 5.

6. I am a two-digit number divisible by 5. The product of my digits is 25.

 **Training Tips**

 Write down all the possible numbers to help.

 Square number = a number mulltiplied by itself

Word problems (+ and −)

Solve these word problems.

1. Read the question carefully.
2. Decide which operation to use.
3. Calculate the answer.
4. Make sure the answer makes sense.

Bronze

1. Sam has 6 sweets and Rob has 5 sweets. How many sweets do they have altogether?

2. I have £12. I am given another £5. How much do I have?

3. 8 people are on a bus. 6 get off. How many people are on the bus now?

4. I have £15. I pay £6 for a cinema ticket. How much do I have now?

5. Three pencils measure 4 cm, 6 cm and 8 cm. If I lay them end to end, how many centimetres would they measure altogether?

6. A ruler is 30 cm long. A pen is 15 cm shorter. How long is the pen?

7. In a box of toy bricks there are 5 red bricks, 6 blue bricks and 7 yellow bricks. How many bricks are there altogether?

Silver

1. Zafar has £6.40. His sister has £4.25. How much more money does he have than his sister?

2. Liam weighs about 100 kg. His brother weighs about 80 kg. How much more does Liam weigh than his brother?

3. 15 girls and 22 boys from Year 5 are going on a trip to the zoo. The journey by bus will take 23 minutes. How many children's tickets for the bus must the school buy?

4. Pop Flops' new CD single is on sale for £2.99. The music shop sold 250 copies on day 1 and 300 copies on day 2. In the same two days Girls Quiet sold 400 copies. Who has sold the most copies?

Gold

1. There are four CD racks. Two of the racks hold 30 CDs and two of the racks hold 45 CDs. How many CDs are there altogether in the racks?

2. What change do you get from £20 if you spend £12.78 on some grocery shopping?

3. Pop Flops played two concerts in August at Wembley Arena. 8120 people came to the first concert and 7845 came to the second concert. How many more people were there at the first concert?

4. The journey from London to Bristol takes 3 hours. The train leaves London at 13:24 but there is a 32-minute delay. At what time does the train arrive in Bristol?

Training Tips

 Check your answers make sense.

 Drawing pictures can help or try imagining the problem.

Word problems (× and ÷)

Solve these word problems.
1. Read the question carefully.
2. Decide which operation to use.
3. Calculate the answer.
4. Make sure the answer makes sense.

Bronze

1. You have 60 litres of water. How many 10-litre buckets of water can you fill?

2. I think of a number and then divide it by 2. The answer is 15. What was my number?

3. A 100 cm tape measure is cut in half. How long is one half?

4. Ice creams cost 10p each. How much will 8 ice creams cost?

5. 6 children sit at each table. How many children sit at 3 tables?

Silver

1. Matt has 25 lollipops. He has 6 people to his party. He wants to give each person 5 lollipops. Does he have enough lollipops?

2. Chad's mum has cooked 16 sausages. How many children can have 2 each?

3. There are 9 cakes on tray. If one falls on the floor and is thrown away, how many can Sarah and Pete have each?

4. Ian buys four books for 60p each. How much change does he get from £5?

5. A shop sold 125 CDs and 86 DVDs in a week. Half the DVDs sold were on special offer. How many special offer DVDs were sold?

Gold

1. Mr White wants 180 eggs. Eggs are sold in boxes of 6. How many boxes of eggs will Mr White need?

2. I think of a number and then divide it by 12. The answer is 6. What was my number?

3. Swimming in a local swimming pool costs £3 for the first hour and £1.50 for every hour after that. How much will it cost for two people to swim for 3 hours?

4. Unleaded petrol costs 75.4p per litre. I put 40 litres in my car. How much do I have to pay?

5. Marcus has 36 sweets. He eats half on Friday and 5 more on Sunday. How many sweets does he have left?

 **Training Tips**

 Check your answers make sense.
Does your answer need units?

 Drawing pictures can help or try imagining the problem.

Number sentences

In every number sentence you are given an operation.
The operation tells you what to do. It is either $+$ $-$ $\times$ or $\div$
In these number sentences the following statements are true:

If $+$ answer is bigger	If $-$ answer is smaller
If $\times$ answer is bigger	If $\div$ answer is smaller

Bronze

a) Copy and complete these with $+$ or $-$

1. 12 ☐ 5 = 17

2. 18 ☐ 6 = 12

3. 25 ☐ 8 = 17

4. 21 ☐ 4 = 25

5. 31 ☐ 7 = 24

b) Copy and complete with $\times$ or $\div$

1. 2 ☐ 6 = 12

2. 20 ☐ 4 = 5

3. 30 ☐ 6 = 5

4. 6 ☐ 6 = 36

5. 5 ☐ 8 = 40

c) Write a word problem for each number sentence:

1. 6 + 5 = 11

2. 16 − 2 = 14

3. 2 × 5 = 10

4. 30 ÷ 2 = 15

5. 24 + 11 = 35

Silver

a) Copy and complete these with $+$ $-$ $\times$ or $\div$

1. 3 ☐ 12 = 36

2. 120 ☐ 4 = 30

3. 52 ☐ 12 = 64

4. 89 ☐ 17 = 72

5. 12 ☐ 10 = 120

6. 54 ☐ 9 = 6

7. 12 ☐ 42 = 54

8. 85 ☐ 42 = 43

9. 5 ☐ 20 = 100

10. 32 ☐ 8 = 4

b) Write word problems for these number sentences:

1. 6 × 6 = 36

2. 24 + 16 = 40

3. 63 − 24 = 39

4. 56 ÷ 7 = 8

5. 263 + 325 = 588

Gold

a) Copy and complete these with $+$ $-$ $\times$ or $\div$

1. 0.2 ☐ 0.5 = 0.1

2. 1.7 ☐ 5.5 = 7.2

3. 15.3 ☐ 1.7 = 13.6

4. 1.2 ☐ 0.5 = 2.4

5. 7.2 ☐ 3.6 = 10.8

6. 0.6 ☐ 1.5 = 0.9

7. 220 ☐ 10 = 22

8. 26.3 ☐ 4.5 = 21.8

9. 5.2 ☐ 0.5 = 2.6

10. 99 ☐ 9 = 11

b) Write a word problem for each number sentence:

1. 11.24 × 3 = 33.72

2. 1468 ÷ 4 = 367

3. 3629 + 4186 = 7815

4. 9283 − 6192 = 3091

5. 121 × 6 = 726

 **Training Tips**

 $+, \times$ **make the answer bigger**
$-, \div$ **make the answer smaller**

 Check your answer makes sense.

Puzzles

Maths can be fun! Use all your maths knowledge to solve these puzzles.

Bronze

Across

1. $4 \times 6 =$

3. $10 + 7 =$

5. $5 \times 10 =$

7. $3 \times 7 =$

9. $6 \times 3 =$

Down

2. $40 \times 10 =$

4. $80 - 6 =$

5. $(100 \div 2) + 5 =$

6. $4 \times 3 =$

8. $10 + 6 =$

Complete this magic square. All the rows, columns and diagonals must add up to the target number. The target number is 15.

	7	
9	5	
4		

Training Tips

Check your answers using reverse operations.

If you are stuck, try to solve a different answer first.

Puzzles

Silver

Complete this magic square. All the rows, columns and diagonals must add up to the target number. The target number is 65.

17		1		15
23	5		14	
4		13	20	22
	12	19		3
11	18	25		9

Across
1. 245 + 119
3. 8 × 3
4. 5264 − 2803
5. 476 ÷ 4
6. 28 × 3

Down
2. 336 + 93
3. 389 − 171
5. 42 ÷ 3
7. 245 ÷ 5
8. 7 × 8

Gold

Complete this magic square with the numbers 1 to 16. All the rows, columns and diagonals must add up to the target number. The target number is 34.

Across
1. 1288 × 3
4. 4379 + 1869
6. 73 × 5
7. 6 × 14459
8. 204963 ÷ 3

Down
1. 1895 − 1571
2. 46857 + 20778
3. 69875 − 23641
5. 12874 + 74100
6. 15904 ÷ 4

Line graphs

Line graphs represent data.
The line graph below shows the change in CD-ROM sales over a year.

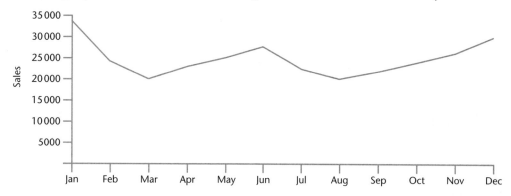

We can see that in February the CD-ROM sales were 24 500 and that in June they were 27 500.

Bronze

a) This graph shows the height of Adrian from when he was born to the age of 15.

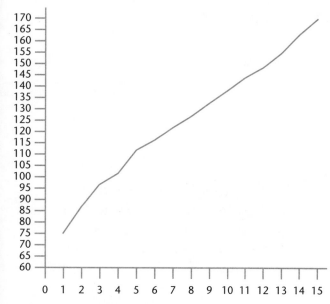

1. How tall was he at 8 years old?

2. How old was he when he was 127 cm tall?

3. How much did he grow between 10 and 13?

4. How tall was he at 10 years old?

5. How old was he when he was 102 cm tall?

6. How much did he grow between 13 and 15?

7. How tall was he at 15 years old?

b) The data below shows the temperature in a greenhouse at different times.

9.00	10.00	11.00	12.00	1.00	2.00	3.00
8°C	12°C	18°C	20°C	16°C	12°C	6°C

Draw a line graph for the information above with a line joining the different temperatures.

Training Tips

Remember to label the axes.
Remember to join the points in the graph together.

Think about the scale to use on your graph before you start.

Line graphs

Silver

a) This line graph shows the average rainfall for each month.

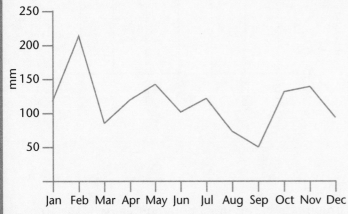

1. How much rainfall was there in March?
2. How much rainfall was there in November?
3. In which month did 101 mm of rain fall?
4. In which month did 143 mm of rain fall?
5. What was the range of rainfall?
6. How much more rain fell in May than in July?
7. What was the difference in rainfall between January and November?

b) The data below shows the price of fish in a market over a year.

Jan	Feb	Mar	Apr	May	Jun	Jul	Aug	Sep	Oct	Nov	Dec
£1.50	£1.60	£1.65	£1.55	£1.40	£1.45	£1.40	£1.50	£1.65	£1.70	£1.80	£1.75

Draw a line graph for the information above with a line joining the different prices.

Gold

a) This line graph shows toy sales in thousands of pounds from January to December.

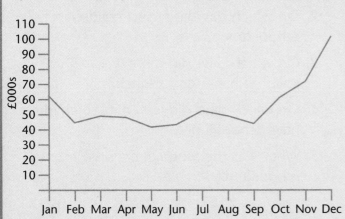

1. How much were toy sales in January?
2. How much were toy sales in November?
3. In which month were £52,500 of toys sold?
4. In which month were £101,500 of toys sold?
5. What was the range of toy sales over the year?
6. How much more in pounds were toy sales in December than in May?
7. How much were the toy sales in August?

b) The data below shows the movement in the price of a sports car.

1990	1991	1992	1993	1994	1995	1996	1997
£35,500	£36,250	£36,000	£36,500	£36,500	£36,250	£36,750	£36,500

Draw a line graph for the information above with a line joining the different prices.

Bar charts and bar line charts

Bar chart

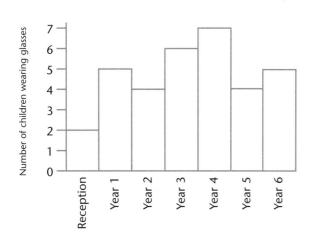

Bar line chart

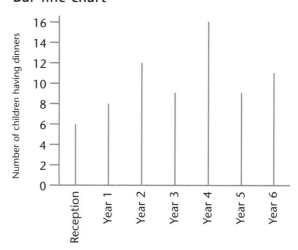

Both these charts are ways of representing data.

Range
The range is the difference between the greatest and the least values.
If a scale goes from 1 to 7, range = 7 − 1 = 6

Mode
The mode is the most common value – the item that appears most often.
We can also call this the modal value.

Bronze

This bar chart shows the number of children in 5T who had school lunch.

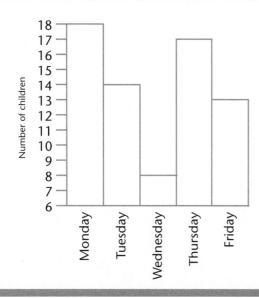

1. On which day did the largest number of children have school lunch?

2. On which day did fewest children have school lunch?

3. On which days did more than 16 children have school lunch?

4. On which days did less than 16 children have school lunch?

5. What was the range of children having school lunch?

Training Tips

Learn what mode and range mean.

Check the scale – does it go up in 2s, 5s, 10s or something else?

Bar charts and bar line charts

a) Ben is raising money for charity. This bar line chart shows how much he raised each day this week.

1. How much did he raise each day?

2. What was Ben's modal amount of money?

3. What was the total amount he raised?

4. What was the range of money he collected?

5. Why do you think he raised the most on Saturday and Sunday?

b) Look at the amount of goals scored by these school football teams:

Churchfields	16	Hollowbank	9
Tilebrook	16	Swallowfield	5
Littlehill	18	Rookbank	16

1. What was the modal score?

2. What was the range of scores?

3. Draw a bar chart for these results.

4. Which teams scored less than 16 goals?

a) This bar chart shows the height of seven children in 5P.

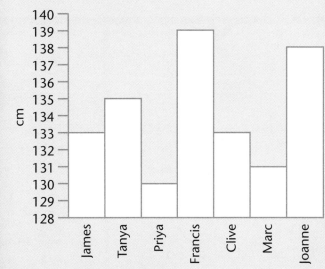

1. How tall is each child?

2. What is the modal height?

3. What is the range of heights?

4. How much taller is Tanya than Priya?

5. Which children's heights are less than 135 cm?

b) This data shows the amount of children who had packed lunch at Haverhill Primary School.

Mon	Tues	Wed	Thurs	Fri
98	9	16	5	18

1. Draw the bar line graph to show this information.

2. What is the modal day?

3. How many more children had packed lunch on Monday than Thursday?

4. What is the range of children having packed lunch?

Probability

Probability tells you how likely it is that something is going to happen.

We can use these words to describe how likely something is:

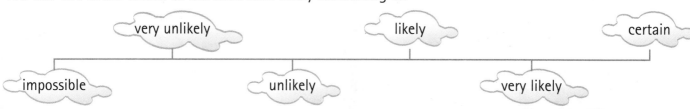

very unlikely   likely   certain

impossible   unlikely   very likely

Bronze

a) It is June and Class 5D go for a walk in a park. How likely do you think each event below will be? Choose from the words above.

1. They will see a dog

2. They will see a tree

3. They will find £100

4. Someone in 5T will fly past them

5. They will see someone in their class

b) Decide which shape is more likely to picked out from each of these bags:

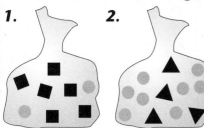

Silver

a) Choose a word from the bubbles to go with each of these events:

1. The first throw of dice will give a 1

2. It will snow some time this week

3. You will go to bed tonight

4. You will become a doctor when you grow up

5. You will learn to fly

b) Place these events on the probability scale above.

1. I will go to the Sun one day

2. I am 9 years old

3. I can talk

4. The Sun will rise tomorrow

5. Now, write your own event for each description on the probability scale.

Gold

a) Draw your own scale like the one above and decide how likely you think each of these events are for you tomorrow:

1. I will watch TV

2. I will see my friends

3. I will go to Spain

4. I will play outside

5. I will win the National Lottery

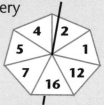

b) List all the numbers this spinner can show if it lands on:

1. a number less than 4

2. a factor of 24

3. an even number

4. a multiple of 2

5. an odd number more than 5

Training Tips

 Impossible – there is no chance of it happening.

 Certain – it will definitely happen.
50:50 – even chance.